MONTENEGRO TRAVEL GUIDE 2020

SVETLANA KRALJ

OPPIAN

Published by Oppian Press
Helsinki, Finland

ISBN 978-951-877-172-5

CONTENTS

WELCOME TO MONTENEGRO!

MONTENEGRO IS A HIDDEN, WILD AND VIVID TREASURE OF Europe. It is on the list among the hottest travel destination. This small country is chosen as one of the top travel destinations, by *New York Times* as one of The Top 31 Places-to-go Worldwide. It was also positioned on a second place in Best in Travel 2013 in the *Lonely Planet* appraisal.

The country is divided into three regions: Coastline, Central Region and Mountain Region on the North. Wherever you go, you will find impressive places. Best of all, it is a well-known and checked fact that in just a few hours you can go from skiing to swimming and enjoy this stunning combination.

Montenegro is recognized as a country of Wild Beauty. Fascinating nature, still untouched by humans, wild and warm at the same time. Five national parks, over 300 km long seashore, lakes, rivers, canyons, mountains, hills, green fields. It can offer even much more: stunning landscapes, beautiful beaches with crystal clear water, churches and monasteries, active holidays in the mountains.

Most of the people who visited Montenegro call it „a piece of heaven on the Earth ". Montenegro is open to all and provides countless opportunities for everyone: whether you are preparing for an adrenaline rush, a serene vacation in villages with a national kitchen, a family vacation, or a desire for luxury. You will enjoy the picturesque countryside, deep canyons, luxury hotels, combined with culture and history, events. Options are inexhaustible and enough reason for Forbes to put Montenegro on a list of must visit a place in 2019. So, if you are still not convinced to travel... Read some opportunities Montenegro offers.

How to reach Montenegro

Montenegro has two international airports and is well connected with almost all destinations. One is in Podgorica, the capital city and second is in Tivat, on the coast. Dubrovnik airport Cilipi, in Croatia, is also an option to consider, because it is only 20 minutes away from the Montenegrin border. Tirana International Airport (Mother Theresa) is 180 km away.

Podgorica Airport, situated 8 km from the city is an ideal choice if you want to stay in the central or northern area. Podgorica Airport is directly connected with almost all major European destinations. The national air carrier of Montenegro is Montenegro Airlines. Other Air Companies that flight to/from Montenegro are: Adria Airways, Air Serbia, Al Italia, Austrian Airlines, Lot Polish Airlines, Ryanair, Wizz Air, Turkish Airlines, Aegean Airlines, TUI as well as many other airlines during the summer season. The flight from/to most European cities lasts from 1 hour to 2.5 hours. The airport code is TGD.

Podgorica Airport is a small but modern Airport. In 2018 they had 2 million serviced travelers.

Rent-a-car offices are situated at the Airport Passenger Terminal, and the offer such as Roksped, SIXT, Ideal, Meridian, Avis, Renault, Europcar and more with a wide range of vehicles for your needs.

Contact details of some of them are:

ROKSPED RENT A CAR: PHONE: +382 (0)69 144 044

+382 (0)69 144 244
Mail: rentacar@rautocentar.com
Web: www.roksped-rentacar.com
SIXT Rent A Car
Phone: +382 (0)67 645 200
+382 (0)67 645 206
Mail: office@sixt.co.me
Web: www.sixt.com

IDEAL RENT A CAR: PHONE: +382 (0)69 888 777

Mail: idealcar@t-com.me
Web: www.idealcar.me
Meridian Rent A Car
Phone: +382 (0)20 234 944
Mail: www.meridian-rentacar.com

AVIS RENT A CAR: PHONE: +382 (0)20 653 066

Web: www.avis.me
Renault Rent A Car
Phone: +382 (0)20 622 914
+382 (0)67 442 775
Web: www.renaultrentacar.com

EUROPCAR MONTENEGRO: PHONE: +382 (0)20 653 141

+382 (0)68 848 400
Mail: reservations@europcar.me
Web: www.europcar.me

Taxi service is situated on the left side of the passenger terminal exit of Airport clearly marked. Taxi counter is on the arrival area. Air-conditioned vehicles are available from Podgorica Airport, during the airport operating hours. The taxi fares are fixed. Ask for the Invoice in a case you need to make a complaint. Also, there is a possibility to book a transfer from the Airport online.

The parking area is clearly marked in front of the Airport building. The first 15 minutes are free of charge. One-hour parking is €0,60 (€5.00 for buses). There is no 24 hours rate, but the monthly parking space is €50.00.

KNOW EXACTLY WHERE ARE YOU GOING

Even though the city looks distant on the map, you do not have to worry about it at all. Montenegro is a small country, and it takes only a few hours to reach one of the airports.

Tivat Airport is smaller than Podgorica Airport and is only 2 km far from Tivat city. Beside National Air Company (Montenegro Airlines), a lot of other companies operate to/from Tivat, such are Air Serbia, Aeroflot, Globus Airlines, Easy Jet, Transavia, Belavia and more at summer. Airport Tivat is the best option for tourist who are planning to stay at the coast. The Airport is very busy during the summer. An important note is that there are no night flights, and in a case of bad weather conditions, flights are diverted to Podgorica Airport with a secured bus transfer to Tivat. Tivat Airport code is TIV.

Car rental service is almost the same as in Podgorica, with Avis, Europcar, Hertz, In Montenegro rent a car, SIXT desk offices.

AVIS: PHONE: +382 (0)32 673 448

+382 (0)68 344 003
+382 (0)32 673 448
Mail: Djani.matkovic@avis.co.me

Web: http://www.avis.com
EuropCar
Phone: +382 (0)32 684 434
+382 (0)68 848 402
Mail: tivat@europcar.me
Web: http://www.europcar.me

SIXT RENT-A-CAR: PHONE + 382 (0)32 540 033

+382 (0)67 645 203
Mail: office@sixt.co.me
Web: http://www.sixt.co.me
InMontenegro Rent-a-car
Phone: +382 (0)32 673 290
+382 (0)67 222 951
+ 382 (0)67 222 065
Mail: info@infomontenegro.com
Web: http://www.inmontenegro.com

HERTZ RENT-A-CAR: PHONE +382 68 882 200,

+382 68 882 205
Mail: tivatap@hertz.me
Web: http://www.hertz.com

Parking service cost €0.80 per hour.

Taxi service is also available in front of the Airport. Tourist should book a transfer in advance. Recommended is to always check a tariff.

Montenegro is connected to Italy by the sea and has operating **ferry boat** that travels several times a week depending on the summer. There is also online booking available with fees and other info.

There is also a **railroad** which connects Montenegro and Serbia (train Bar-Beograd) and regular **bus lines** toward Serbia, Croatia, and Macedonia, as well as between cities in Montenegro.

Air:

- Airport Podgorica:
- Phone: +382 (0)20 444 244;
- Airport Tivat
- Phone: +382 (0) 32 670 930
- Mail: info@apm.co.me
- Web:http://www.montenegroairports.com

Ship:

- Line Bar-Bari, Bari-Dubrovnik
- Barska plovidba, Bar
- Phone:: +382 (0)30 303 469; +382 (0)30 312 366 Mail:online@barplov.com; booking@barplov.com
- Web :http://www.montenegrolines.net

Railroad:

- Phone:
- Podgorica +382 (0)20 441 211/2; Bar +382 (0)30 301

615; Sutomore +382 (0)30 601 690; Nikšić +382 (0)40 214 480; Mojkovac +382 (0)50 472 130; Bijelo Polje +382 (0)50 470 560; Kolašin +382 (0)20 441 492;

- Web: http://www.zcg-prevoz.me

HISTORY OF MONTENEGRO

THE RICH AND DRAMATIC HISTORY OF MONTENEGRO HAS LED to the creating of a heroic and knightly codex, which is still present today among the people. Montenegrin history is so full of wars but yet so full of freedom and struggle for the same. Every place and every part of Montenegro has its own story.

Before the arrival of the Slavonic peoples in the Balkans during the sixth century AD, the area now known as

Montenegro was inhabited principally by the Illyrians. The Greeks, the Celts, and the Romans have lived on the territory of Montenegro over history. These cultures have influenced the Montenegrin tradition, but not much as the arrival of Slavs. The Slavs settled in the area of Duklja and fought constantly against Byzantium.

Before the ruler (Slavic: Knez) Vladimir at the end of the 10th century, there was a little source about the Duklja and its rulers. Rulers Petar and Jovan Vladimir established their own state. However, at the end of the 9th century, they fell under the reign of Emperor Samuel, and then under the Byzantine empire.

Vojislav liberated Zeta (from that time Zeta began to replace the old name Duklja) from Byzantine control in 1042, and his grandfather Bodin helped the growth of the Zeta who then controlled Raska, Bosnia, and Skadar. After Bodin's death, the state had another fall under the Byzantine empire, and in 1185 it was under the state of Raska.

In the second half of XIV century Zeta gains independence from the central Serbian state, first under the rule of the Balsic Dynasty and later Crnojevic Dynasty, and starts existing as an independent feudal state. Ivan Crnojevic leaves the capital in Zabljak and moves to Cetinje in 1482 where he builds the monastery in 1484, which becomes the center of Zeta metropolis (diocese). Djuradj Crnojevic was the last ruler of medieval Zeta; he established a printing press in Cetinje in 1493, in which *Oktoih the first voice* (*Oktoih prvoglasnik*) was printed, first Cyrillic printed book of south Slavs. After a very short Djuradj's rule, Montenegro falls under the Ottoman Empire in 1496.

Montenegro fought four centuries against the Turks. Montenegrin tribes have long been divided and could not give more resistance. In 1696, Danilo Petrovic was elected the prince-bishop of Montenegro, he succeeded in establishing peace among the tribes. During the reign of Sava, a breeding quarrel appeared again. After Sava and Vasilije death, the self-proclaimed Scepan Mali appeared; presented himself as Emperor Peter III in Russia and imposed himself as the ruler of Montenegro. But shortly thereafter, Petar I Petrovic Njegos assumed spiritual and secular control over Montenegro and formed the first joint government of Montenegro and Boka and issued the first law called *Stega*.

His nephew Petar II Petrović Njegoš abolished the administrative system, introduced the captains' courts, the Senate and the first secular school in Montenegro. He brought a printing press in Montenegro and influenced the cultural and economic growth of Montenegro. Petar II Petrović Njegoš was the last prince-bishop who had secular and spiritual authority. His successor, Danilo I Petrovic, separated the secular and spiritual authority and made a new code.

The greatest rise of Montenegro occurred during the reign of Prince Nikola I Petrović Njegoš (1860-1918). At the Berlin Congress in 1878, Montenegro was recognized as completely independent and began to recover both culturally and economically. In 1905, Prince Nikola adopted a Constitution. The National Assembly crowned him as king in 1910 and proclaimed Montenegro a kingdom.

During the First Balkan War, the territory of Montenegro expanded greatly and after the end of the First World War, Montenegro united with Serbia and came to the Kingdom of Serbs, Croats, and Slovenes, and later Yugoslavia.

In the year 1941, Montenegro was occupied by the Nazi

troops and both German and Italian soldiers remained there. Almost 10% of the Montenegrin population died to occupational forces, from nationalist and fascist formations from the interior of the country, and also revolutionary and ideological clashes during the liberation war. Montenegro becomes one of the six people's republics of Democratic Federative Yugoslavia under the strong leadership of Josip Broz Tito.

After President Tito's death, inability and unpreparedness of each republic's leadership to open the way to political reforms and to face the question of preservation or abandonment of Yugoslav federation in a democratic way, lead to SFRY's breakdown resulting in a bloody civil war at the beginning of the 90s.

In 2006 Montenegro again becomes the independent Republic of Montenegro. At this time Montenegro is negotiating about accession to EU.

CULTURE

When asked about the country's culture and tradition, the first answer would be ethics and courage. These two words perfectly summarize the entire Montenegrin tradition. The history of Montenegro is full of wars and struggles, and the Montenegrin people are known for their strong freedom of will, heroism, and deep ethical principles. History and tradition are inextricably linked to each other and ethical ideal of humanity and bravery is an important part of Montenegrin culture.

Language and Literature of Montenegro are a rich part of

the country's culture. One of the oldest scripts *Miroslav Gospel (Miroslavljevo jevandjelje)* dates back from the first half of XII century. Being written for Prince Miroslav of Hum, it is decorated with around 300 colorful miniatures and initials, decorated with stylized flora and fauna, and various other ornaments. Miroslav Gospel is the most significant Cyrillic monument. *The Chronicle of the Priest of Duklja* (Ljetopis Popa Dukljanina) a work of an anonymous writer, was written in the second half of the XII century. One of the most beautiful parts of the Chronicle refers to the cross of St. Vladimir, which has been kept by the family for a long time on the edges of Bar. This cross is part of the tradition of each of the three religions from Montenegro: Orthodox, Catholic, and Islamic; they are presented once a year at the highest point of Mount Rumija (in Bar).

Interesting facts:

- Montenegro is a multicultural, multiethnic country of freedom, where people can express themselves no matter which cultural or religious background they have. The main religion of the country is Orthodox Christian and most of the people are Montenegrin. Besides that, there is a high percentage of other nationalities living in Montenegro (Serbians, Bosnians, Croatians, Albanians, Macedonians, etc.) while Orthodox Christian, Catholicism and Islam are among most widespread religions.

Montenegro's literary tradition dates from early times and it is a rich part of a country's culture. The first printing press in Montenegro was founded in 1493, only 40 years after the founding of Gutenberg's press. It was founded by Djuradj Crnojevic, last medieval ruler of Zeta. Located in Obod near

Rijeka Crnojevica, this printing house published five books, one being *Oktoih the first voice, (Oktoih prvoglasnik)*, first Cyrillic book of Southern Slavs. Oktoih, the first voice was printed in 597 pages, in two colors and decorated with figural compositions and renaissance initials. The beauty of the technique of Crnojevic's printing house to this day delights the historians of the book.

The biggest traces of baroque art of Montenegro are found near Perast, in Church of Our Lady of the Rock. The Bay of Kotor's school of painters gave a noticeable figure to European iconographers and fresco painters from Risan.

At the beginning of the XVI century, one of the most striking figures of the medieval culture of Montenegro made an appearance, printer Bozidar Vukovic Podgoricanin who brought our book to European cultural circles.

Montenegro has three big symbols: Cetinje, Njegos, and Lovcen. From its founding and up to 1946, the city of Cetinje was the capital of Montenegro, the center of all main cultural and historical events. In fact, the whole of Cetinje is a kind of museum. In it, aside from a first state elementary school, first state high school was founded—Bogoslovija, also Djevojacki Institut (Institute for Women) and first higher education institution in Montenegro. More famous buildings are Biljarda, King Nikola's Palace, hospital Danilo I, Government House, Blue Palace.

During the time of Petrovic dynasty, a big influence on the development of social thought was Cetinje Monastery, a famous spiritual and literary center. Almost all rulers from Petrovic dynasty were writers as well, the most important ones. They wrote epistles and chronicles in a language filled with folk wisdom of wars of Montenegrins. Such writer-rulers were: Petar I Petrovic Njegos (1747-1830) known for his *Epistles (Poslanice)*. Vasilije Petrovic Njegos (1706-1766) wrote *History of Montenegro* which was published in Moscow in 1744.

Petar II Petrovic Njegos (1813-1851), aside from being a bishop was the greatest poet in the literary history of Montenegro and South Slavs. His most famous poems are *The Ray of the Microcosm (Luca Mikrokozma,* 1845), *The Mountain Wreath (Gorski vijenac,* 1847) and *False Tsar Stephan the Little (Lazni car Scepan Mali,* 1851). Njegos became the ruler of Montenegro in his eighteenth year. Besides writing great literary works, he founded a first secular school in 1834 in Montenegro, built a printing house and made cultural development progress faster. He died in his thirty-seventh year of life and was buried according to his wishes on top of Lovcen, 1 660 meters high.

King Nikola I Petrovic was also a writer. His most famous work was a drama *The Empress of Balkans (Balkanska carica).*

In Montenegrin literary history, there aren't many people whose life's work can be so closely compared to their literary life as is the case with Marko Miljanov (1833-1900). His most famous work is The Examples of *Humanity and Bravery (Primjeri cojstva i junastva)* in which he talks about the ethical and moral value of Montenegrin people and historical hazards.

In the literary history of Montenegro significant place belongs to Stefan Mitrov Ljubisa (1824-1878) who wrote two books of short stories: *Stories of Montenegro and the Littoral (Pripovijesti crnogorske i primorske, 1875)* and *Storytelling of Vuk Dojcevic (Pricanja Vuka Dojcevica,* 1877-1879), and his most important story is *Kanjos Macedonovic.*

Interwar, war and post-war literature have many important

names while modern literature has seen a long line of well-known names, winners of many important awards and tributes.

The big success of Montenegrin culture in the world was aided by painters. Milo Milunovic, Petar Lubarda, Dado Djuric, Cvetko Lainovic and Vojo Stanic are just a few from our great line of artists. The Academy of Arts in Cetinje continue to grows up new talents.

Manifestations in Montenegro are a very special place for many cultural creators from the country and world to gather. Most of them take place during the summer months in coastal towns. Some of the manifestations are *Theater City Budva (Grad Teatar Budva), Bar Chronicle (Barski ljetopis), Herceg Novi Book Fair, Tivat cultural summer, Summer scene in Ulcinj, Festival of theater for children in Kotor,* and much more.

The traditional Montenegrin folk music instrument is called **gusle**. Traditional folk dance is called Oro, and it is a dance in which players stand in a row leaning against one another on their shoulders while one or two players stand in the middle. Yes, you read it well – stand on each other's shoulders.

In Montenegro, modern sport is cherished; it is a result of many centuries of knight games. Montenegrin royal court and diplomatic missions greatly helped in the development of sport in the Kingdom of Montenegro. Near the end of XIX century in Montenegro football, tennis and golf were played and also ice-skating, skiing, fencing, cycling, and horse riding was represented as well. At the beginning of the XX century, first clubs were formed in the aforementioned sports.

Interesting facts:

- Montenegrin National costume is one of the most beautiful in the World. Many young people decide to get married in National clothes rather than in wedding dresses or suits.

FESTIVALS & EVENTS

In addition to natural beauty, Montenegro has much to offer in terms of festival, event, nightlife. During the summer, all nightlife moves to the sea. Many tourists are surprised to see the parties every night or the day of the week! On the beach, pool, open bar, anywhere.

In Montenegro, there are clubs, dance festivals and events to suit every taste.

Open beach bars, pool parties, clubs, traditional events, and Festivals – you will find it all here.

The most crowded city is Budva. In search of nightlife, lovers of good entertainment will surely choose Budva. Unquestionably. The guaranteed best choice for spending time without limits.

Casper in Old town is beautifully decorated bar under the olive tree where DJs are spinning and also hosts own **Jazz Festival. Greco café** is filled to the last place and is the busiest place in Old Town. **Torch**, beach club, bar, and restaurant have an amazing concept, outdoor party, pool parties. **Club Ambiente**, is outdoor with theme parties and Dj's. **Discoteque Budva** is a popular indoor club. **Opera club**, located above the beach Jaz, with live acts is very crowded. **Dukley Beach Longue** is the oasis in Zavala with the original concept and breathtaking horizon view. **Omnia Night Club** and Paris **Night Club**, on the main promenade offer the best fun in the city. It is impossible not to mention **Club Top Hill** with capacity up to 5000 people, on open air, hosting the big DJ's. Sound and light experience and sea view from the top of the hill makes this place so popular.

Sea Dance Festival – is award-winning International music Festival, which extends of EXIT Festival (Novi Sad). It was held on Jaz beach since 2014th and on 2017th is relocated to Buljarica Beach (15 min ride from Budva). Traditionally hosting the biggest names of the Music Scene.

Not only Budva but other sea cities have a rich nightlife. The most popular club in Kotor is **Maximus**, situated in fortress inside Old City. Almost every genre of music is presented, with modern equipment and an unforgettable experience.

Maximus also host traditional **Refresh Festival**, with several stages and different genres which attract visitors from all around the globe. The energy of this Festival is unseen.

A lot of events, parties are in the area around Ulcinj. **The Southern soul festival** – is a multi-day festival at Ada Bojana, traditionally brings together people from all over the world which became a must-be-there place for an unforgettable experience. Soul, jazz, funk, and house live acts on the sandy beach.

A lot of open clubs and bars which offer day and night parties along with Ada Bojana. **Dolcinium Kite club** at Copacabana Beach, **Gecko club** on the Velika plaza.

Traditional **Lake fest** and **Bedem fest** are Festivals which are happening every year in Niksic. Lake Fest is located on the Lake Krupac, near the Niksic and takes 3 days on open air and free camping space. This festival attracts mostly rock music lovers. Bedem fest within the walls of the Niksic bedem fortress.

A **City Groove Festival** is a traditional, electronic music festival happening in Podgorica.

Not all tourists who visit Montenegro at the same time are fans of loud music from clubs, or it is not their vision of a vacation. Montenegro has much to offer - concerts, literary evenings, exhibitions, book fairs, performances, theater.

Kotor is a host of **Kotor Art International Festival.** It is one of the biggest and most important festivals. Every summer, an impressive number of international artists gathers, with over 200 programs at numerous ambient locations in Kotor and around Boka attracting tens of thousands of visitors, which makes it one of the most visited festivals of this type. It's happening at the end of July and beginning of August each year.

In Podgorica, **Podgorica's cultural summer (Podgoricko kulturno ljeto)** is a traditional manifestation which takes part from May to September and held open cinema, theater plays, and concerts.

Bar city is a host of summer cultural event called **Bar's chronicle (Barski ljetopis).** It includes theatre, art, literature, classical music, book fair.

Days of Music (Dani muzike) take place in Herceg Novi in July. It is a classical music festival.

International Fashion Festival takes place in Kotor. The guests are great designer names such as Dolce & Gabbana, Prada, Armani, and many others, as well as fashion designers from Montenegro, managers, actors, celebrities.

International summer carnival (Kotorski maskenbal)

brings entertainment in the streets of Kotor. There is also a winter version of the carnival.

Boka-night (Bokeljska noc) is a tradition of two centuries. Then the boats floating through the Kotor Bay are decorated, dancing and singing and ending with a large firework.

Budva city theater (Grad Teatar) is a cultural event in July and August, known for its open theater and musical performance.

In Petrovac, near Budva, the traditional **International Petrovac Jazz Festival** is held in late August.

This event list is not complete. It is impossible to mention everything; the best advice is to follow the leaflets or check on the official website of Montenegrin tourism https://www.montenegro.travel/en

LOCAL CUISINE

Montenegrin cuisine depends on the geographical position because the dishes served on the shore differ from the meals in the northern mountainous regions.

On the coast, there is a great influence of Mediterranean cuisine, along with the usual seafood dishes (fish, octopus, shrimp, and squid). It is based on large quantities of fresh fruits and vegetables, low-fat meat and fish. You will feel the influence of Italian cuisine not only on the coast but also in preparing pasta, bread, vegetables, cheese making.

In the northern part, the food is continental, stronger, with the influences of the cuisine of the people that were less or more in this region.

Any part of Montenegro to visit, you will get healthy, organic food.

Whenever we travel to a country, we ask ourselves what kind of national food is and what can surprise us. Montenegro is ready to surprise you, offering you national dishes. One feature that should never be forgotten: Montenegrins are magnificent hosts. You will always get the best place at the table and the best the host can offer. Montenegrin national food opens your way - taste it with love!

Common welcome Montenegrins will show with **priganice** served with honey, cheese or jam. Priganice are fritters or flat donuts.

Before any dish, there is **prsuta (smoked ham)** and sir (**cheese).** There are almost no house, restaurant, the hotel where is no prsuta and sir. This is the first thing that every host will serve you. Speaking about cheese, you will find many kinds of them. Except for **njeguski sir** (usually served with njeguska prsuta) popular is **kolasinski sir,** layered, white cheese.

The golden yellow circles of the famous njeguski cheese are kept in a cold placer up to 3 months before tasting. Rich in milk fats, this cheese is a delicacy of Montenegrin national cuisine.

With a glass of homemade wine, a piece of smoked cheese and olives, this cheese will best prove why it's special.

Seaside is famous for sea specialties. Important notice: fish is always fresh. Most restaurants will show you fish before preparing it for you.

Black risotto is usually served with seafood. Black color gets from the cuttlefish ink.

Shrimps, clams, squid, prawns, octopus salad with a lot of different vegetables are well-known at the seaside homes and restaurants. That food is usually served with vegetable **blitva** (chards) or boiled potatoes.

Similar to blitva is **rastan** an extremely delightful dish of vegetables from the cabbage family, cooked with white potatoes. Minced meat rolled in green leaves of rastan gives a Montenegrin specialty: **japraci.** It is a must try dish.

With green vegetables, cheese, potatoes or minced meat, you will get famous pies. The most popular is the **burek.** A glass of yogurt with it is a must!

Either on the coast or on the north, **cevapi** are popular everywhere. Cevapi is a widely popular grill and maybe a reason why there is no McDonalds in Montenegro.

Kajmak is cheese cream made from unpasteurized, unhomogenized milk. It's usually served with bread as an appetizer, or with meat. On the North of Montenegro, you can find aged kajmak which is usually much stronger, but taste good.

Meat is widely popular. One dish that you will try only in Montenegro is **njeguski steak.** It's a veal or pork steak filled with smoked ham and cheese or kajmak.

Kacamak is a dish you must try. Kacamak is a traditional food made of made of buckwheat, corn flour, potato, adding kajmak and served with milk. It is a must try while at North.

Cicvara as well has a wonderful taste - truly softens in the mouth.

Popara - by blending a bit of bread with drain oil and cheese, is profoundly established in Montenegrin sustenance.

Cooked potatoes are light and most loved supper, which is joined by cheese and yogurt.

Sweets are coming after food but before coffee. From pancakes to cakes, ice-cream or fruit salads sweets are a must in Montenegro.

It is trusted that the Montenegrins are great and kind hosts who, as an appreciated welcome, open the doors of their home, they put it "at the leader of the table" and offer the best food and drink. On the table, at that point, there is smoked ham, cheese, boiled eggs. This, as an hors d'oeuvre, until the point that it is primarily food heated or cooked.

ACCOMMODATION OPTIONS

WHETHER YOU ARE A BACKPACKER, A HOSTEL LOVER, A CAMPER or a luxury hotel guest - Montenegro will gladly welcome you and offer the accommodation you are looking for.

If you plan to visit Montenegro on a **budget,** then look for catch cost flights for Montenegro. There are Ryan Air, Wizz Air, Easy Jet and if you book your flight in advance, you can get a one-way ticket for 9.99€. You can mix and match different airports to reach your destination.

Whatever city you choose for your destination in Montenegro, keep in mind you can go from mountain to coast for several hours. The best option for accommodation is staying in a hostel. Each of them has friendly staff, a home atmosphere and before going to nightlife, a night break with **rakija** and music. There is a possibility for a free bike in some hostels. Be careful if you first drink rakija. It's a strong alcoholic drink, and it's easy to get drunk.

Alternatively, you can rent the entire apartment or room. Besides Airbnb, Booking.com and other websites, you will see signs for the room/apartment rent. Do not be afraid to stop and ask for accommodation. Apartments and rooms are not limited to the duration of your stay - you can even rent it for one day.

Renting a bike is a good idea to save time and money.

Talking with locals is better than paying for an overpriced tour. Montenegrins are kind people, always ready to give advice or offer the best solution. In this way, you can easily get a new friend.

Buy food at local markets and stores. Montenegro is famous for its domestic fruits, vegetables, cheese, and other products. If you can cook in a hostel or rented apartment, you will save a lot of money.

Street food is everywhere. Hamburger usually costs about 2€, pancake 1.5€, pizza 1-2€, sandwich 1-2€. In the bakery, ask for a **burek** with yogurt or a piece of pizza. Bread is also cheap, less than 1€.

Choose beer **Niksicko pivo**, a local beer instead of more expensive beer. There is no regret here. Many bars have Happy hours or promotional drinks, be sure to check them.

Buy a SIM card. In Montenegro are several mobile operators offering good packages and thus avoiding expensive roaming calls. Avoid taxi if you are on a budget. There are free entries for many sights, museums, exhibitions. Just try to ask around.

If you come to Montenegro and want to experience the country like a **local**, then you do not need travel books and guides. When you are at Montenegro Airport, have several local taxis ready. Official airport taxes are expensive and, in this way, you will save more than half the price. Check the price before you enter the cabin. If you go to another city, use a bus or train to transfer. Everyone in Montenegro will tell you where the bus or train station is located and how to get to it.

Do not believe every hotel review you can see on the internet. Have a list of places you want to explore. Buy a map, use a Google map or navigation. In almost every place you can come by yourself, faster and cheaper.

If you see a bar or restaurant full of foreigners that don't mean you have to sit or eat there. Instead, try to eat where local people eat. You will recognize them by language. Or simply ask the locals for your favorite restaurant. Try homemade food. Montenegrin food is a mix of the Mediterranean and Turkish food. **Cevapi, burgers, prsuta, sir, kajmak, burek, muckalica, popara** - don't be afraid of this food, even on the street.

Have a good evening dress for evening outings. Montenegrins like to dress well, so don't come in flip flops in a club, for example.

Learn customs and culture, even better learn words like **hvala** (thanks), **zdravo** – (hello), **zivjeli** (cheers) and connect with local people who are very friendly to you. Greet people with three kisses. Friendships created in Montenegro remain forever and memories from this stunning country.

If you want to travel **in style**, pack bags full of modern clothes. Every year, an international fashion festival is held in Kotor, where you can see the Montenegrin designers, as well as Armani, Versace, Prada, Dolce & Gabbana and many other collections and celebrities.

The choice of destinations will probably be *Dukly Hotel & Resort* in Budva, with a beautiful view of the sea and a private beach. Or Regent Porto Montenegro in Tivat with a view. Hotel *Aman Sveti Stefan* is also on the list for an unforgettable experience or *Splendid Conference & SPA Resort* in Becici with stunning beach views and a magnificent swimming pool. Among the many excellent hotels, we recommend *Hotel Majestic Budva, Hotel Moskva Budva, Forza Tera, Forza Mare in Kotor, Hotel Zia Podgorica, Podgorica Hotel Hilton, Centreville Podgorica, Four Points Sheraton Kolasin, Iberostar Perast,* hotels and villas *La Perla Petrovac, Hotel Regent Porto Montenegro.*

Merit Casino Royal is one of many casinos in Montenegro. It is located in the *Splendid Hotel, Becici* and the most famous of the films by James Bond recorded in 2006. The luxurious places and restaurants are not just on the coast. Wherever you go through Montenegro, make sure you find the accommodation and services you are looking for.

If you are traveling in search of a **romantic place** with your loved one, Montenegro has the ideal place to offer.

The perfect escape to a quiet place is Montenegrin mountains and ethno villages in which you can feel freedom and tranquility. A bungalow or cottage surrounded by the scent of pine trees, and a friendly host that will serve an organic breakfast and you are ready to explore the beauty of the North with your second half. There are many places to mention several ethno villages of *Nevidio, Milogor, Goles, Komneniva, Vukovic,* who will make your stay unforgettable. There are many organized tours and events to enjoy.

In the Bay of Kotor, a small place Persat will take your breath away with its idyllic beauty. A romantic dinner with slow music by the sea will make magic. We recommend booking apartments in advance because Perast is small and has limited accommodation.

In almost every city in Montenegro, it is very easy to find a romantic part, even with chill-out music, live instrumental music or relaxing piano music.

USEFUL INFORMATION

- Currency in Montenegro is Euro €
- Tome zone is CET (Central European Time) UTC/GMT +1 hour (+2 at summer)
- The official language is Montenegrin
- Information about visa system can be found on the website of Ministry of Foreign Affairs of Montenegro; web: http://www.mip.gov.me
- Calling code for Montenegro is +382
- There are three mobile network operators: Telenor (069), T-Mobile (067), Mtel (068).

Calling codes of cities in Montenegro:

- 030 Bar, Ulcinj
- 051 Berane, Andrijevica, Plav, Rožaje
- 050 Bijelo Polje, Mojkovac
- 033 Budva
- 041 Cetinje
- 031 Herceg Novi
- 032 Kotor, Tivat

- 040 Nikšić, Plužine, Šavnik
- 052 Pljevlja, Žabljak
- 020 Podgorica, Danilovgrad, Kolašin

Note: if you are calling from Montenegro, drop +382; if you are calling from abroad drop 0 before the city code

Public Holidays:

1-2 Jan – New Year's Day

6-7-8 Jan – Orthodox Christmas Days

Apr – Orthodox Good Friday (movable)

Apr – Orthodox Easter days (movable),

1-2 May – Labor Days,

21 May – Independence Day

13 July – Statehood Day

Transportations:

Airports:

web: http://www.montenegroairports.com

Podgorica: (+382) 20 444 244

Tivat: (+382) 32 670 975

Train stations in Montenegro:

web:http://www.zcg-prevoz.me/

Podgorica: (+382) 20 441 211, 441 212

Bar: (+382) 30 301 615

Sutomore: (+382) 30 601 690

Nikšić: (+382) 40 214 480

Mojkovac (+382) 50 472 130

Bijelo Polje: (+382) 50 478 560

Kolašin: (+382) 20 441 492

Bus stations in Montenegro:

Podgorica: (+382) 20 620 430

Herceg Novi: (+382) 31 321 225

Kotor: (+382) 32 325 809

Tivat: (+382) 32 627 620

Budva: (+382) 33 456 000

Bar: (+382) 30 346 141

Ulcinj: (+382) 30 413 225

Berane: (+382) 51 243 828

Bijelo Polje: (+382) 50 432 219

Pljevlja: (+382) 52 323 114

Nikšić: (+382) 40 213 018

Cetinje: (+382) 41 21 052

Ships:

web: http://www.montenegrolines.net/

Barska plovidba: (+382) 30 303 469; 312 366; 312 366;311 465

Embassies and consulates in Montenegro:

Albania: St. Stanka Dragojevica 14, Podgorica (+ 382) 20 667 380

Austria: Bul. Svetog Petra Cetinjskog 1A / VI Podgorica (+ 382) 20 201 135 / 201 136;

Bosnia and Herzegovina: Atinska 58, Podgorica (+382) 20 618 015; 618 105; 618 135;

Bulgaria: Vukice Mitrovića 10, Podgorica (+382) 20 655 009;

France: Atinska 35, Podgorica (+382) 20 655 348; 655 344;

web: www.ambafrance-me.org

Greece: Atinska 4, Gorica C, Podgorica (+382) 20 655 544; 618 170

Croatia: Vladimira Ćetkovića 2, Podgorica (+382) 20 269 760;

Italy: Džordža Vašingtona bb, Podgorica (+382) 20 234 661; 234 662;

web: www.ambpodgorica.esteri.it

China: Radosava Burića 4a, Podgorica (+382) 20 609 275; 609 285; 609 295;

Macedonia: Hercegovačka 49/3, Podgorica (+382) 20 667 415; 667 416; 667 206;

Hungary: Kralja Nikole 104, Podgorica (+382) 20 602 910; 602 880;

web: www.mfa.gov.hu/kulkepviselet/ME/HU

Germany: Hercegovačka 10, Podgorica (+382) 20 441 000;

Poland: Kozaračka br. 79, Podgorica (+382) 20 608 320; 20 608 321;

web: www.podgorica.polemb.net

Romania: Vukice Mitrović 40, Podgorica (+382) 20 618 040; 618 041;

web: www.ambasada.podgorica.go.ro

Russian Federation: Veliše Mugoše 1, Podgorica (+382) 20 272 315;

United States of America: Ljubljanska bb, Podgorica (+382) 20 410 500;

web: www.podgorica.usembassy.gov

Slovakia: Crnogorskih serdara 5, Podgorica (+382) 20 601 440;

web: www.mzv.sk/podgorica

Slovenia: Atinska 41, Podgorica (+382) 20 618 150;

web: http://podgorica.embassy.si

Serbia: Hercegovačka 18, Podgorica (+382) 20 667 305; 667 565;

Turkey: Radosava Burića bb, Podgorica (+382) 20 445 700;

United Arab Emirates: Bulevar Sv. Petra Cetinjskog 147, Podgorica (+382) 20 411 401;

United Kingdom of Great Britain and Northern Ireland: Ulcinjska 8, Gorica C, Podgorica (+382) 20 618 010 web: www.ukinmontenegro.fco.gov.uk

Ukraine: Serdara Jola Piletića br.15, Podgorica (+382) 20 227 521;

Important numbers:

Automobile Association of Montenegro: 19807; web: http://www.amscg.org

Information about telephone numbers: 1181

Police: 122

Firefighters: 123

Emergency room: 124

Survival phrases:

Good morning – Dobro jutro

Do you speak…? – Da li govorite…?

Good afternoon – Dobar dan

I don't understand – Ne razumijem

Good evening – Dobro vece

How do you say…? – Kako kazete…?

Hello – Zdravo

I am looking for… – Trazim...

Bye – Cao

Do you have a map? – Imate li mapu?

Goodbye – Dovidjenja

Could I see the menu? – Mogu li vidjeti meni?

See you later – Vidimo se

I need a doctor – Treba mi doktor

Thank you – Hvala

Call the police! – Zovite policiju!

Sorry – Izvinite

I am tourist – Ja sam turista

How are you? – Kako ste?

How much is it? – Koliko kosta?

Fine, thanks – Dobro, hvala

Cheers! – Zivjeli!

Yes – Da

No – Ne

Shop – Prodavnica

Bank – Banka

What is your name – Kako se zoves?

Entrance – Ulaz

My name is… – Zovem se.,,

Exit – Izlaz

BOSNIA AND HERZEGOVINA
SERBIA
Pljevlja
Bijelo Polje
MONTENEGRO
Kolašin
Berane
Rožaje
Nikšić
KOSOVO
CROATIA
Herceg Novi
PODGORICA
Tivat
Kotor
Cetinje
Lake Skadar
Adriatic Sea
Bar
Ulcinj
ALBANIA

THE COASTLINE

Let's start our trip by exploring the South Coast of Montenegro. There are two beautiful cities, Bar and Ulcinj.

BAR

Bar is located on the south of Montenegro, and it was mentioned in the 6th century for the first time. Today, it is a modern city between the Adriatic Sea and Lake Skadar. Its central part is a mountain massif of Rumija, Sozina, Sutorman, and Lisinja which also makes nature border between the Adriatic Sea and Lake Skadar. As a port-city, Bar is connected by water with shores of the Mediterranean Sea and ports from all continents.

Bar is 46 km away from Podgorica airport and 59 km from Tivat airport. It is easy to connect with other cities by local bus, train or by the ferry from Italy (Bari). The first encounter with Bar for all those who did not come to this part of Montenegro is like a surprise! The combination of the smell of salt and amazing wine is spread through the whole city and makes the stay even more pleasant. In the city center, you will find modern houses, bars, wide streets, and souvenir shops. A few steps further you will see marina, next to other modest boats and expensive yachts. However, the water is turquoise, the blue color of the crystal clear water is a true diamond of Bar.

The buildings of King Nikola I Petrovic is located near the shore in Topolica and comprises of a Great castle, a Small castle, Sentry tower, Chapels, Winter Gardens, and The Great Park. Even if there is no precise information about when this complex was built it is assumed, they were built in 1885 by an architect from Trogir, dr. Josip Slade. Today this complex is used for purposes of **Heritage museum** of Bar and other cultural uses. Also, there is a Restaurant called *Knjazeva Basta*. Walking down the main Square, visitors usually try the best ice creams in Montenegro.

Old Bar is the biggest urban agglomeration in Montenegro. In Old Bar, the neighborhood Podgrad is found, which dates from medieval ages but is also populated today. There are several old taverns, shops, workshops and local market worth to visit as well mosques and Catholic Church of St. Marry in Podgrad.

In a Mirovica, a settlement near Bar many famous olive trees are located. **The Old Olive Tree** (Stara maslina), a symbol of Bar is more than 2 000 years old.

Most of the beaches are located at a distance greater than 2 km from the city center. It is very easy to reach them, either by tourist organized transportation, boat taxi or public transportation.

Bar is a host of many cultural events. **Barski ljetopis** is a cultural festival which over 30 years promotes culture and valuable art content bringing together eminent creators from Montenegro, the region and the world.

Interesting facts:

Bar is one of the sunniest cities in Southern Europe. The number of sunny days a year, on average, is 270. Bar climate is known for long and warm summers and mild winters. There are few real winter days. Snow and frost during winter are rare.

When you visit the Old Olive Tree, the legend says to turn around Old olive tree 3 times – for the happiness, health, and love.

The best souvenir from Bar is a bottle of domestic Olive Oil.

Best beaches are located outside of the Bar.

Kraljičina plaza (Queen beach) is one of the most attractive beaches covered with the finest sand. It is a small sheltered bay separated by high rocks, which can also be accessed only from the sea.

Canj beach, or Pearl beach, colorful send surrounded by pines and cypresses.

Veliki pijesak beach is 10 kilometers away from Bar to Ulcinj. It is a sandy beach with a beautiful sunset.

Crvena (Red) beach is a beach between Bar and Sutomore named after the extreme red color of the sand or stone pebbles.

Must visit:

- **Old Town** - There are two small museums inside.
- **King Nikola's Palace** – breathtaking buildings and park; small fee entrance for the museum inside.
- **Church of Saint John Vladimir** – located in the city center, amazing interior, and small souvenir shop. No photos allowed inside.
- **Old Olive Tree** – located near the Old Bar, Mirovica Bar, direction to Ulcinj, best to visit together with
- **Old Fortress, Stari Bar** – beautiful scenery, and great food
- **The Aqueduct** – part of the stone arch bridge supported by 18 stone pillars.
- **Visit Skadar Lake** - 20 min from Bar.
- **Explore Queen beach** – called after queen Milena, King Nikola's wife, a yacht only exclusive beach.
- **Sutomore** originates from 1882 when the first houses were built on the coast. Sutomore has a long, sandy beach and many Bar visitors prefer to enjoy the beach there. In the summer, hotels are usually overbooked, but it is very easy to find private accommodation at reasonable prices. Sutomore has a

lot of attractive restaurants, terraces with live music, beach bars, clubs, and tourists have a lot of fun.

- **Virpazar** - To escape from summer heat, for a day or more, take a road to Virpazar, a famous tourist spot for cruising around Lake Skadar. Virpazar is a small and quiet fishing settlement and main trading center of Crmnica area, famous for the vine, olives, fruit. In it, there are many crafts, boats and tourist taxi boats which generally operate in the summer and organize tourist cruises around Lake Skadar. Spending a day or more there would be memorable to explore Skadar Lake and its beautiful scenery. Definitely, Virpazar is a spot for taking breathtaking photos.

USEFUL INFORMATION:

- Bar has a good choice of restaurants with fresh seafood, domestic and international cuisine.
- There are all kinds of accommodations. Comparing with Budva it is must cheaper.
- Train station: Bar: (+382) 30 301 615 Sutomore: (+382) 30 601 690
- Bus station: (+382) 30 346 141
- Marina Bar: (+382) 30 315 166; web: http://www.marinabar.org
- Port: Barska plovidba (+382) 30 303 469; (+382) 30 312 366; http://www.montenegrolines.net
- Tourist organization of Bar: (+382) 30 311 633; web: http://www.visitbar.org
- Cultural center Bar Promenade of King Nikola (+382) 30 313-810

- Heritage museum King Nikola's Castle (+382) 30 315-355
- Open for visitors every day from 9 - 14h and 18h - 20h
- Art Gallery Velimir E. Leković: ul. Jovana Tomaševića 57 (+381) 30 315-998
- Hospital Bar Podgrad bb - Stari Bar tel: (+382) 30 342-209
- Medical Center Bar, Jovana Tomaševića 42, tel: (+382) 30 311-001
- Police Bar 122
- Emergency room 124

ULCINJ

Ulcinj is located in the southern part of the Adriatic coast. Part of the coast that belongs to Ulcinj is considered the most valuable part of the Mediterranean. Through the southern part, with 30 km long Ulcinj is connected with the Adriatic Sea. On its east river, Bojana flows and connects it to Albania. There are also fields with lakes, swamps, small rivers, and long sandy beaches. The central part of Ulcinj is covered with Sasko Lake, while the bay itself is surrounded by the massif of mountain Rumija.

According to historical data, Ulcinj is certainly one of the oldest cities on the Adriatic coast. It is considered that Ulcinj is more than 2,000 years old. Cultures of Orient and the West have collided in this area for centuries, which, according to the richness of the historical heritage, is felt at every step. As the traces of the first settlements in Ulcinj occur in the 5th century BC, it is considered that Ulcinj was founded by the Illyrians, a nation of Indo-European origin. At the time of the free Illyrian state, Ulcinj also experienced the greatest bloom. The original name of Ulcinj was the Colchinium, and it was given after the Kolhydians (a tribe of Greek descent), which are considered to be the founders of the old Ulcinj core. In Ulcinj until 163 BC, Illyrian tribe Olciniatas ruled and then they were conquered by the Romans in the 2nd century BC. At that time, the ancient Colchinium becomes Olcinium (Ulcinj).

Due to the exceptional geographical position, mild climate and relief, Ulcinj was for centuries the target of the conquerors. During the Roman Empire, Ulcinj was given the status of a city with special privileges (Opida civium romanorum), so that later Ulcinj would become a city with an independent status, or - Municipium. After the division of the Roman Empire, Ulcinj belonged to the Prevalis Province, which was an integral part of the Eastern Empire, and the population became Christian.

Ulcinj is very well connected with other cities by car or by bus. You can use 4 airports to reach Ulcinj: Podgorica (77 km), Tivat (85 km), Tirana (125 km) and Dubrovnik (136km). You can use a train to come to Bar and continue with a bus to Ulcinj (28 km).

Ulcinj with its surroundings belongs to the subtropical zone of the European Mediterranean area. Such climate provides much warmth and sun, with 270 sunny days a year, which means that Ulcinj is one of the sunniest places on the Montenegrin coast. A majority of the population of Ulcinj is ethnic Albanian.

Old Ulcinj is located on the southernmost part of the Montenegrin coast. The first settlement in this place was founded at the end of 4th or at the beginning of 5th century BC when many Illyrian settlements were built along the Montenegrin coast. In the 12th century, Ulcinj became the most famous maritime town on the Adriatic. The main attractions in the Old town are the town museum and the views.

Ada Bojana is a river island. Ada Bojana is in the shape of a triangle with the river Bojana from two sides and the Adriatic Sea from the third one. From one side it touches the Adriatic Sea and from the other side touches river Bojana. Beach that faces the sea is sandy and 3 km long. Nearby you can find restaurants, sports terrains, parking lots and various sports activities like horseback riding, sailing, windsurfing, and riding in paragliders. Island is decorated with subtropical and Mediterranean overgrowth.

Sasko Lake is located near Ulcinj. It is unique in beauty, clear and peaceful and very rich with fish. On the lake and its surroundings, you can find around 240 different species of birds: storks, herons, geese, wild ducks, cormorants. A lot of migratory birds on their long journeys to southern parks stay on Sasko Lake, which attracts ornithologists from all parts of Europe, so the bird watching became very popular kind of recreation in Ulcinj. On Sasko lake remains of an ancient city, Svac or dead city were found, which was conquered by Mongols.

Cove Valdanos is located five km north-west from Ulcinj. The cove is surrounded by olive fields from all sides. There are also very nicely arranged pebble beaches made out of large pebbles.

During the summer Ulcinj is a lively place with lots of tourists who like to get off the beaten track. With the firm establishment of kite surfing here, it's also become a popular place for young travelers who want beach parties but are looking for a more underground destination than Budva. One of the biggest kitesurfing resorts is located precisely on Ada Bojana in Ulcinj.

Ulcinj is very famous for its sandy long beaches and beautiful sunsets for the whole year. There are good beach spots in the area. A lot of beaches host day and night parties, Festivals, Kite surfing, and other activities. The biggest festival held on Ada Bojana is called **Southern Soul Festival** and it gathers people from all around the World each year.

Interesting facts:

According to the legend, the famous Spanish writer Cervantes, in his young age, was in Ulcinj as a slave of pirates and his *Don* Quixote is linked to this imprisonment. A statue of Cervantes is in Old City.

The cultural development of Ulcinj is also important, with a large number of names responsible for its flourishing.

Due to a large number of parties and festivals, Ulcinj is called Balkan Ibiza.

Best beaches:

Ada beach is 2.600 m long. Restaurants, camping houses, a nudist resort on the island, coastline specificity: sailing, paddling, hunting, fishing and other water sports. There is also a Nudist Beach at Ada Bojana.

Mala plaza is a sandy beach next to the old town. This beach is popular with families because it's sandy and shallow.

Zenska plaza or Lady beach is a well-known remedy for infertility.

Kite Surf beach

Tropicana beach

Valdanos Cove and many more sandy and rocky beaches for anyone taste.

Must see:

- **Old town**
- **Ada Bojana**
- **Valdanos Cove**
- **Sasko lake**

DON'T MISS:

- **Southern Soul Music Festival.** Traditionally held 6-day International festival of world's leading soul, jazz, funk and house live acts, and DJs together with the most unique and beautiful setting of the longest sandy beach on the Mediterranean coast, Velika Plaza. Every year, the festival brings together a large number of foreign and domestic music lovers and provides an unforgettable experience. There are nonstop day and night parties.
- **Ada Bojana.** Ada Bojana is a place far from the city noise where it is surrounded by pure natural beauty. The two sides are conveyed by the river Bojan, and the third by the sea. Ada Bojana is one of the most

popular tourist destinations of Montenegro for many years, and one of the most interesting attractions is a 2880 meters long sandy beach. One thing you should not miss is the sunset. Many couples decide to get married at Ada Bojana on sunset.

Directions: Ada Bojana is located about 10 km from Ulcinj and can be reached by car/taxi/ bus.

USEFUL INFORMATION:

- Hotels, restaurants, bars that offer good food and entertainment are everywhere. Seafood, national food, every kind of food with cheaper prices than in other coastal cities. Activities such are sailing, fishing, paragliding, diving, camping offers a lot of possibilities.
- Kite suffering is very popular and there are schools for suffering lessons.
- Horseback riding on Ada Bojana is a real adventure.
- Bus station: (+382) 30 413 225
- Heritage Museum: Old city (+382) 30 421 419 for visitors open during summer, entry fee 2 €.

BUDVA

The vast majority of people heard about Budva. It is a city that has a record attendance year after year, the most visited destination in Montenegro. It attracts tourist all over the world with its beautiful beaches, sceneries, historical monuments. It is the perfect choice for anyone who wants to feel an attractive day and nightlife.

The city of Budva is the center of Riviera and one of the oldest settlements in the Adriatic region. Budva has a population of 19 218 and to determine the number of tourists who visit is almost impossible. Swimming season lasts from the middle of May until the middle of November. Budva Riviera has a total area of 122km^2.

There are 35 amazing beaches on Budva Riviera, most of them with a blue flag. Whether you're seeking solitude or a party vibe, crystal clear water or sun shade – you will find them here.

The Old Town is a trademark of Budva. Its walls date back to the Middle Ages when the Venetians ruled this area. In the Old Town, there is also a city fortress dating from the V or VI century before the new era, which today is a stage of the famous City Theatre. In the fortress, there is the church of St. Ivan, built in the 7th century, which builds St. Mary in Punta from 840, and another church St. Trinity from 1804, also in Citadel. The **City Museum** of Budva is located in the Old town. It is an archaeological and ethnographic museum which covers the town's history from prehistoric times to the 20th century.

The climate of Budva is the typical Mediterranean with very warm summer and mild winter. Budva is full of restaurants, bars, nightclubs, events, festivals for everyone taste. Due to numerous bars and nightclubs, it is a favorite destination of the young. The YouTube channel is full of videos of Budva nightlife. Girls and guys are following the latest fashion trends. A lot of expensive cars, motorcycles, exclusive yachts, trends are seen by day and night.

Budva is also an important cultural center, and it has been since many centuries. Many cultural manifestations are held in Budva annually, and the biggest one is called **Grad Teatar Budva** (City Theatre). It is held during summer and the Festival hosts numerous theater, opera, ballet troupes from all around the World. Many archeological spots that prove the existence of life on the territory of Budva, even during the ancient period. There are many stories and legends about the building of Budva. Stefan the Byzantine (6th century) reported the most authentic legend about the foundation of Budva, and, until today, this legend is the most famous one. The legend says that Cadmus, a hero from Boeotia and founder of the town of Thebes, left his homeland in order to search for his sister Europa. Europa was taken away by Zeus, and Cadmus was sure to find her. However, he was unsuccessful in his wish to find his sister, and then consulted the Delphic oracle. Delphic oracle ordered Cadmus to give up his quest, follow a cow and build a town on the place where the cow lays down. The place where the cow laid down was Boeotia, and Cadmus founded the well-known city of Thebes there. There, he ruled for many years with his wife Harmonia. Cadmus and Harmonia were expelled from Thebes in their old age and they had to move. During their move, they found a new town called Budva (Bouthoue). According to the legend, graves of Cadmus and Harmonia are somewhere on the territory of Boka Kotorska or Drac. The history of Budva is very interesting and still unexplored in details. More of these visitors are able to hear during their guided tours through Budva.

Budva is a pearl of Mediterranean for a reason. You can't say you visited Montenegro if you didn't visit Budva during the summer.

10 must-visit beaches:

Mogren Beach – actually two sandy beaches connected by a short tunnel in a rock. It is far only 150 meters from Old town.

Richard's Head (Ricardova glava) – small beach between the Old Town and Avala Hotel. It got a name by actor Richard Widmark who filmed "The Long Ships" in Budva in 1964.

Jaz beach – Lonely Planet's number 1 beach. It is mostly sanded and pebble, the 4 km long beach with open sea view. Also famous for award-winning festival Sea Dance which is moved to **Buljarica** Beach.

Kamenovo beach – is located 6 km from Budva. Also famous for Spring Break Festival. There is a small bus running every 15 minutes from Budva to Becici and cost €0.50-1.00 one direction.

Ploce beach – the beach is located next to Jaz beach, 6 km from Budva in Direction to Tivat. It is a pebble beach with several pools, restaurants, and lounges. It is a famous party beach.

Pizana – the small beach inside the Old Town. It is popular and usually overcrowded.

Guvance beach – is a small beach and part of Dukley

Gardens, located near the tunnel towards to Becici.

Becici beach – the most popular, clean, long beach. This sandy beach has a lot of facilities. In the background is a complex tourist resort.

Przno beach – is a mix of sand and rock, 8 km from Budva and a 1-minute walk from Maestral Resort & Casino. It is situated in front of the vivid, typical sea shore settlement, which gives the beach a special charm.

Queen's Beach – is a part of Sveti Stefan Aman Resort, so only guests of the hotel can enjoy this beautiful beach as well as Milocer beach also known as King's beach, for guests of Aman Sveti Stefan.

Interesting facts:

At the Mogren beach entrance is the bronze poured ballerina. The sculpture became a symbol of Budva and is one of the main tourist attractions. There is no tourist and even a local who at least once did not take a photo near the famous Mogren ballerina.

The sculpture is inspired by an old local legend. She was a girlfriend of the sailor who sailed away a long way to earn for living together with her. He never returned, and the girl remained faithful to him and came to this rock every morning to watch the sea.

She has been waiting for him for years until one morning they found her dead on the rock where the famous statue is today.

Must visit:

- **The old town, Citadel** - small but beautiful with restaurants and boutiques selling luxury goods.
- **Dancing Girl statue** – on a way to Mogren beach to make a memorable photo with a view on Old town.
- **Aquapark** – situated on the Toplis Hill.
- ***Beer and Bike club***, part of restaurant *Jadran kod Krsta.*
- **Jaz beach**, only a few km from Budva, Lonely Planet's 'The best beach in Europe 2015'.
- **Top Hill Club** for dancing all night long. (Location Toplis Hill)

Tips:

Music finishes at 1 AM in most open-air clubs and restaurants.

There are a traffic jam and a long wait for parking.

Be aware of taxi price, always check fare before you start a ride.

Not allowed to eat in restaurants in beach clothes.

Accommodation:

Probably the best hotels in Montenegro are on the Budva Riviera. Here you will find large hotels with casinos, pools, and views of the sunset. Budva has more high-rise hotel complexes than any other Montenegrin city.

Numerous tourists opt for private accommodation by renting rooms or apartments, villas, hostels.

From luxurious 5-star hotels such as Splendid Conference &

SPA Resort, Dukley Gardens, Tre Canne, to apartments such as Alexandar Montenegro Luxury Suites, Montelux Apartments, to Avala Resorts and Villas, Hotel Majestic or Montenegro Hostel Budva to name a few – there is plenty accommodation for any taste and budget.

If you want to be close to the city, but you are looking for a more peaceful place to relax, you will find them in the small places along the Budva Riviera.

Becici is a part of Budva Municipality, located only 2 km from Old Town. It is separated from the main area in Budva by the narrow peninsula Zavala where exclusive landmark with **Dukley Hotel & Resort** is situated. The beautiful, pebble beach is almost 2 km long. It is among the most beautiful beaches in the southern Adriatic. The area is loaded with different activities and offerings, even for the most imaginative visitors. Surrounded by cypress trees there is a small Orthodox Church St. Toma.

It is easy to reach Becici from Budva by walking or by minibus on their route to Petrovac and St Stefan.

Becici offers are various options for accommodation: from private accommodation in rooms or villas to superb hotels, including the famous 5-star Hotel **Splendid Conference & Spa Resort**, where part of the James Bond movie Casino Royale was filmed.

By the end of Becici, opposite direction from Budva, there is an old fisherman village **Rafailovici** with pleasant cafes and restaurants.

Petrovac is also part of Budva Riviera. It has excellent accommodations, lots of extra activities, beautiful beaches, crystal clear sea water, playgrounds. Petrovac is an ideal place for a family vacation. Beautiful beaches are Lucie and Buljarica, in which Sea Dance Festival is held.

DON'T MISS:

- **Island St. Nikola** also called Hawaii. This is the largest Montenegrin island, less than 1 km far from Budva. the island is covered by many conifers, pine, and spruce forest. It has very versatile wildlife, roe deer, rabbits, and many rare plants. You can reach the place by boat taxi (leaving from Slovenska plaza) or renting a kayak.

Once you arrive at the destination, you will find the clear sea, blue sky, sun rays and the smells and tastes of the Mediterranean. One-day excursions to the island offer swimming, exploring or enjoying the sea, the peace and the Mediterranean.

- **Sea Dance Festival** – electronic and pop music festival 5th edition, this year moving from the Jaz Beach to Buljarica Beach over 2 km long with seven stages (15 min ride from Budva). The Sea Dance Festival brings together fans from around the world and an impressive lineup that of the world's most popular music stars. For the past four years it has been held on Jaz beach and since 2018 it was moved to the Buljarica beach.

Many world media, including CNN, New York Times,

Guardian, Conde Nast, Metro, Daily Mirror, Daily Express, and others, recommend Sea Dance as one of the world's best seafront festivals.

- **Sveti Stefan.** The island of Sveti Stefan, with its rich history and beautiful nature, is among the most beautiful jewel of Montenegro. It is connected by land with a narrow causeway. Former fishing town located on the islet turned into city-lodging, a magnificent place which hosted celebrities from all over the world, statesman, a playground for the rich and famous: Sofia Loren, Carlo Ponti, Kirk Douglas, Doris Day, Geraldine Chaplin, Sylvester Stallone, Yuri Gagarin, Bobby Fischer, Princess Margaret and King Umberto II to name a few. This is the most extravagant summer resort in Montenegro and is the most prominent place on the Adriatic. Also, the most photographed site.

Now it is privatized by Aman Resorts and closed for visitors. You can't access the island unless you're a hotel guest. But you can get onto the island with a restaurant reservation. The north beach is for hotel guests while the south is free for the public. The prices here are higher than elsewhere on the coast. Sveti Stefan is on the list of TOP 10 Glamorous sites of the World (A-List) by Lonely Planet choice.

Directions: It is 6 km from Budva, so you can reach it either by car or public transport that goes from Budva to Petrovac. You can visit Sveti Stefan also from Petrovac/Bar direction to Budva.

. . .

USEFUL INFORMATION:

- Bus station: (+382) 41 456 000
- Museums, gallery, library of Budva: st. Petra I Petrovica 11, Old town (+382) 33 453 308
- Modern Gallery: Cara Dušana 15, Old town (+382) 33 451 343
- The archeological and ethnographic museum, Old town (+382) 33 453 308 33;
- Activities: paragliding, aqua ski, bungee jumping, diving, excursions...
- Many tourist agencies offer different arrangements for anyone taste.
- Variety of fish restaurants famous for fresh fish, national and international cuisine, pizzerias and pastries, winery, grills
- Clubbing and nightlife guide: http://www.budvanocu.com/en

BOKA BAY

The Boka Bay or Bay of Kotor as the only fjord in the

Mediterranean was included in one of the 25 most beautiful fjords of the world in July 2000. From artists to tourists, everyone experiences it as something special, unusual, wonderful. Boka Kotorska is on the list of World's natural and cultural heritage of UNESCO.

Boca is located under the cliffs of Lovcen and Orijen. In one part, the mountains are raised from the calm surface of the sea, and in the second part there are botanical gardens and places such as Njivice, Igalo, Herceg Novi, Savina, Meljine, Zelenika, Kumbor, Baosici, Bijela, Kamenari, Morinj, Risan, Perast, Ljuta, Kotor, Prcanj, Tivat, Krtole, Krasici, Radovici, Rose. Boka is decorated with seven beautiful islands. In spring, when the mountains around the bay are still covered with snow, at the foot of the mountains fruit trees begin to blossom and flowers to bloom. That is a reason Boka has a specific climate, quite specific to the rest of the Montenegrin coast.

Boka Bay has a rich and long history and culture since the ancient period until modern time. For this reason, Boka is the starting point for an acquaintance with Montenegro and its historical core. You will rarely come across such a beauty that will leave you breathless.

The total area of the bay is 87.3 km and the length of the coast is 105.7 km. It is recommended to take a tour around the Bay. You can find tour operators and rentals along the waterfront with options ranging from a half hour to the entire day. The breathing sceneries are at every step.

Directions: You can reach Boka by

The main road through the road: Bar - Budva - Tivat / Kotor; Niksic - Risan; Trebinje - Herceg Novi; Dubrovnik - Herceg Novi.

By the plane via the airport in Tivat, Dubrovnik, and Podgorica.

By the sea via the ports in Kotor and Herceg-Novi.

KOTOR

Kotor is *Lonely Planet's* number one destination for 2016. It is located t the top of the bay and is a UNESCO World Heritage Site and a medieval fortified town. From the east, it is surrounded by the slopes of Mount Lovcen and the hill of Sveti Ivan, in the southwest, it is connected to the world by the sea. Kotor is the largest old urban area in Montenegro. He preserved the medieval schedule of narrow streets, city squares, palaces, churches within the mighty city wall, which stretch along the edge of the hill of St. Ivan to his top.

The walls of Kotor are about 4.5 kilometers long and up to 20 meters high. It is not known exactly when the walls were built, but the fact that they were growing in parallel with the expansion of the city. Although they attacked it several times, the Ottomans never entered in Kotor because of the powerful walls.

The Old Town

The Old Town is the most famous part of Kotor. Almost all history, churches, cathedrals, palaces, and museums are located inside. Also, the cultural monuments such are Tower watch (VIII century), Cathedral of St Tripun (XIII century), Church of St Luka (XIII century), Prince's palace (XVII century), Church of St Marija (XII century), Church of Our Lady of Health (XV century), and Napoleon's Theater (XIX century). The Old town is shaped roughly like a triangle and has 3 entrances, the main one is the Sea Gate.

The town itself is a combination of restaurants, shops, apartments and visiting spots. Cars cannot get into the old town so the best way to explore it is a walking tour. If you take a wrong turn you will wind up far from your destination. Information kiosk in front of the entrance is selling the maps. But Old town is not big, even you get lost you will find a way out.

St Trifun Cathedral is located in Old Town. It was built in honor of St Trifun, the city protector and patron. It is a Roman Catholic cathedral which contains a rich collection of artifacts. It is the symbol of the Kotor city.

Maritime Museum is located also in Old Town in the baroque palace Grgurin. It is a long running museum with nautical history exhibits, including model ships, paintings & furniture.

Beaches in Kotor are not developed. Namely, recognized as a city of only cultural significance, Kotor has been in this direction for centuries and has developed, so the number of beaches is small and stone. In places Orahovac and Ljuta there are two very small sandy beaches.

Due to the unique mix of different cultural influences, Kotor was listed in the World Heritage List under the protection of UNESCO in 1979. Kotor is one of the few cities where, from year to year, many traditional events are held that attract a large number of domestic and foreign tourists: *Bokeska noc,* Traditional Kotor *Carnival, Festival of Camellia, Kotor Children's Theater Festival, International Fashion Show* and many others. A lot of bars, clubs, restaurants, nightclubs are filled to the last place. Kotor is Montenegro's must-see destination. Kotor is a popular port for cruisers. Cruise ships arrive daily between April and November and the streets are alive with tourists and locals alike.

Must visit:

- **The Old Town**
- **San Giovanni Fortress Walls** - climb up 1,350 steps (approximately 45 minutes each way) to enjoy the magnificent view and take beautiful photos.
- **Churches**
- **City Walls and Fortress**

Tips:

It's easy to get lost in Old City – mark your starting point.

Get a map on Information desk at the main entrance.

For ladies: very hard to walk wearing heels.

Cats of Kotor – a souvenir, and donation.

Hostel people in Kotor have unique experience.

Accommodation

Whether you want to stay in Baroque hotels, inside or outside of the old town, the choice is great - from 5 stars villas and luxury hotels to private accommodation and popular hostels.

DON'T MISS:

- **Perast**. Perast is one of the most beautiful places in Boka Bay, about 12 km away from Kotor, where the Kotor and Risan Bay are separated. Perast is a small town with very beautiful and colorful architecture. In the center of the city, there is a square (Pjaca) where you will find the church of St Nicholas with its impressive 55 meters high bell tower. Perast is under UNESCO heritage protection.

Perast can only fit a certain number of people. There are only four hotels in town and a limited number of apartments available, so early booking is recommended. A bad location is not possible in Perast. Because of the lack of beach zone, the coast of Perast is not suitable for beach tourism. The place is quiet and ideal for dinner, and sea view. It is easily reachable by car or local bus. There are no sidewalks so consider it if you are thinking to go from Kotor to Perast by walk.

- **The Island Gospa od Skrpjela (Our Lady of the Rocks)**. If you look from Perast to the Bay of Kotor, you will see two islands that seem to swim on the sea surface, unrealistic and beautiful, Gospa od Skrpjela and the island of St Djordje (St George). Our Lady of the Rocks (built in 1630 by Venetians) is an island visited by numerous explorers; the most outstanding artwork is kept there, and it was partly made, for a long time, by Jacinta Kunic-Mijovic while sitting tight for her cherished one to come back from the ocean. Other than brilliant and silver filaments, she used her own hair in making the woven artwork. You can get a tour visit to the church and the museum for a very small fee. The tour usually takes about 30 minutes, so plan your ride back 45 minutes (more or less) after the moment you arrive. Take some time after the tour to enjoy fascinating scenery of the Bay.

Directions: You can easily go to both islands by boat (the fee is usually 3-5euros per person).

USEFUL INFORMATION:

- Kotor is fairly well connected with neighboring cities by local buses
- Bus station: (+382) 32 325 809
- Tivat airport is 8 km away
- Port Kotor:(+382) 32 325-208
- Harbormaster:(+382) 32 325-578
- Maritime Museum of Montenegro – Old City: (+382) 32 325 646
- Heritage Museum of city Perast: (+382) 32 373 519
- Cathedral of St. Tripun, Old City 336
- Our Lady of the Rocks, Perast (+382) 69 013 678
- Church of St. Nikola, Perast
- Activities: sailing, mountaineering, diving, nautical, dancing
- Seafood, national cuisine, authentic food, pastries,

wine, soft drinks, coffee... everything is located in the Old town.

- A night out in some of the many open bars within the walls of Old town or in club Maximus with DJs and live music
- Kotor is rich with events especially during the summer
- Emergency room: 124

TIVAT

Tivat is city located in the central part of Kotor Bay. The city is suitable for relaxing in winter and summer thanks to clean air, favorable climate, and rich vegetation. There is an international airport which is 3 km from the city center.

In the history of Boka Kotorska, the following epochs are clearly distinguished: the Illyrian, Roman-Byzantine, Serbian, Venetian, Ottoman and Austrian. The shores of the Tivat Bay passed through all these epochs, as seen by many archaeological finds, and existing monuments of old architecture. There are many cultural and historical monuments: **The complex of the monastery of St Arhandjela Mihaila** (St. Archangel Michael), **Otok Gospe od Milosti** (the Gospel Isle of Grace), many of churches, renaissance summer house **Buca** and others. There is an interesting consulate: The Consulate of SFRY (ex Yugoslavia).

A lot of cultural and entertainment events are happening in Tivat, such are Bokeljska *noc* in Donja Lastva, *Youth Day* (Dan mladosti), *Tivat Cultural Summer* (*Tivatsko kulturno ljeto*),

November Days of Culture (Novembarski dani culture) and others.

As a touristic destination, Tivat has its expansion in the last several years. It is 15 minutes from Kotor and 30 minutes from Budva. As a small town, it can be explored by foot. On the Tivat Riviera, there are 17 beautiful beaches, which can satisfy even the most demanding guests. Accommodation vary from beautiful hotels and villas to private accommodation.

Top beaches

Plavi Horizonti (Blue Horizons) situated in the open sea, sandy beach ideal for families with small kids and for non-swimmers because the sea is very shallow.

Oblatno - **Almara Beach Club** is a hotspot for young and trendy. The beach is located on Lustica peninsular and has luxurious sun loungers with baldachins. It is a party beach with DJ's and loved by young people.

Movida beach is a part of the Movida Restaurant and Lounge Club. It is a spacious beach covered with pebbles with performances of international DJs and regional music stars.

Waikiki beach is located in Seljanovo is a sandy pebbled beach international cuisine & drinks, lounge, terrace, and amazing children playground.

Must visit:

- **Buca house**
- **Botanic garden**
- **Gornja Lastva**

- **Ostrvo cvijeca (Flower's Island)**

DON'T MISS

- **Porto Montenegro.** It is the top luxury place in Europe. Porto Montenegro is more of a city in itself offering everything a spoiled visitor would want. The superyacht Marina was rewarded as one of the best in the overpopulated Mediterranean part of Europe. An evening stroll along the waterfront is a must.

Porto Montenegro is not only an exclusive marina and yachting place. It consists of luxury residences, waterfront serviced apartments, Yacht Club and Regent Hotel. The place offering exceptional events for all ages and tastes.

USEFUL INFORMATION:

- Tivat is full of water-based activities, hiking, biking, bowling, and other activities.
- Luxury restaurants in Porto Montenegro or Tivat promenade has plenty of good eateries to choose from. Italian influence on food is noticeable.
- Tivat, the town has a lively nightlife scene all year around.
- Airport Tivat: (+382) 32 670 960, (+382) 32 670 975, web: http://www.montenegroairports.com
- Bus station: (+382) 32 672 620
- Museum collection and gallery Tivat, st. Nikole

Đurkovića 10, (+382) 32 674 590, (+382) 69 342 799; web: www.czktivat.co.me

- General consulate SFRY: st. Palih boraca 4, (+382) 67 291 143 web: http://www.konzulatsfrj.com

HERCEG NOVI

This beautiful city is known for its good climate, flowers, and stairs. Herceg Novi is a city on the edge of the Bay of Kotor. The city's appearance is a mixture of Romanesque, Byzantine and Oriental style enhanced with Mediterranean charm. As in other cities on the coast, as well as in Herceg Novi, the mild Mediterranean climate with dry warm summers and mild winters is present. The swimming season in Herceg Novi lasts for up to 5 months.

The city has a developed flora, and especially flowers, which is also called *The City of Flowers*. The sailors contributed to this, who, returning every time from the distant seas, brought new plants. So is the flower of mimosa, brought even from Australia. Mimosa bloom at the beginning of February and, every year, the famous manifestation Days of Mimosa is held.

The Herceg Novi Riviera is 25 km long and includes settlements **Meljine, Bijela, Djenovici, Kumbor, Zelenika**. The Herceg Novi Riviera is best seen from the Orjen mountain, which is 1895 meters above sea level. Herceg Novi has a well-organized mountaineering society, and the road that can climb to Orjen is well marked. Apart from walking, jeep safari is an option to visit Orjen.

Fortresses within the walls of the **Old Town** (Spain, Fortress,

Forte Mare, Kanli Kula) with many palaces and churches testify to the old town spirit.

Characteristics of the Old Town of Herceg Novi are stairs, visitors and tourists are often difficult to climb. The old town is surrounded by a wall built in the 5th century. In addition to Forte Mare and the Kanli Kula, it is recommended to visit two large squares in the Old Town: Trg Herceg Stjepan, National Library, Art Galleries, City Archives.

There are also very beautiful, officially around 70 registered beaches, mostly concrete platforms with sandy parts, which extend from Njivice to Macak Cape on the peninsula Lustica.

Best beaches are:

Savina, Dobrec, Rose, Zanjice.

Must visit:

- **The Old town** is the beating heart of Herceg Novi located just above the town's marina.
- **The clock tower** located in the Old Town, built by the Ottomans in the 17th century.
- **Kanli Kula** built in the 16th century is a great spot to get panoramic views of the whole of the Herceg Novi coastline.
- **Savina Monastir** which is 15 min walk from the Old town

DON'T MISS

- **LUSTICA BOAT TRIPS.** The beautiful Lustica peninsula is also possible to visit, and you can book a day trip by boat. You will have the opportunity to visit the island of Mamula, which was once a prison. You will also find Blue Cave, a hidden gem of Montenegro, and swim in the most beautiful beaches.

USEFUL INFORMATION:

- Day trip to Dubrovnik, Croatia (distance is 50 km).
- Driving tour around Boka Bay – definitely will take a breath away, a lot of places to stop and take stunning photos
- Try mud therapy at small spa and health center Igalo
- Bus station: (+382) 31 321 225
- Heritage Museum: Mirka Komnenovića 9, (+382) 31 322 485; web: http://www.rastko.rs/rastko-bo/muzej
- Working hours 9-17, entry fee 1 €, for students' entrance is free
- City library: square Hercega Stefana; web: www.bibliotekaherceg-novi.org.rs
- Monastery Savina, st. Manastirska 21, open for visitors 6 – 20 h, entry is free.
- Numerous sports clubs, diving centers, paragliding.
- Hotels, restaurants, bars, pizzerias, clubs offer numerous entertainment content.

Maybe you would like to explore the central region of Montenegro? Let's start!

Explore Central Region

CETINJE

Cetinje is Old Royal Capital of Montenegro and one of the smallest cities in the country (with only 16 657 inhabitants). Although a small city, it is often considered to be the heart of Montenegro. Cetinje is located halfway between Podgorica and Budva, right in the center of the main road leading from the capital to the sea (31 km from Podgorica, 29 km from Budva). This place feels and looks like an actual city-museum, and a part of the country that is a must visit.

Cetinje has a long tradition of being a historical and cultural center of the country. For more than four and a half centuries, this city was the capital of the country, a place where all important things were happening. The city was founded in the fifteenth century, by Ivan Crnojevic, who moved his former capital (Zabljak Crnojevica) due to frequent clashes w1ith the Turks and Ottoman Empire. Ivan Crnojevic wanted to find a suitable ground and territory that was difficult to encircle and approach, so the area on which Cetinje is located today was an excellent choice for such intentions. In 1482 Ivan Crnojevic built himself a palace in the Cetinje field, and two years later the monastery, today is known as **Cetinje Monastery**.

Cetinje Monastery, which dates back to 1484, is one of the symbols of Cetinje, but also of the whole Montenegro because it shows the persistence in its full attire. The monastery was completely destroyed by the Ottomans in 1692 but also restored not far from its original location, by Bishop Danilo. During this rebuilding, stones from the old monastery were taken and embedded in a new monastery, as well as the slab with the crest of the Crnojevic dynasty. In the 18th century (1712), the monastery was again attacked and burned by the Bosnian vizier Ahmet Pasa but restored only 30 years later by the Montenegrin metropolitan Sava Petrovic Njegos. However, the monastery was burned again in 1785 from Mahmud-Pasa Busatlija, but Petar I Petrovic Njegos renewed it. The contemporary appearance of the monastery dates back to 1927 when it was minimally restored. Even though this monument was attacked several times, it resisted both attacks and time passing. The importance of the Cetinje Monastery is also visible in everything that is kept in there. Among the most famous is the hand of St. John the Baptist, for which many tourists from all over the world come to the Monastery.

Besides being a spiritual center, Cetinje became the secular center of the country, a cultural place that positioned Montenegro on the top of cultural life in the 15th century. Đurađ Crnojevic, Ivan's son, founded the **first Cyrillic printing house** in 1492. This was the first printing house in the South Slavic region and also one of the first in the whole of Europe. For more than four centuries, Cetinje continued to be a cultural and educational center of the country. Even today, Cetinje is an important cultural place in Montenegro. **National Museum of Montenegro** is located in there, and it is consisted of 4 independent museum units: **Historical Museum of Montenegro** (composed of the King Nikola Museum, Museum of Petar II Petrovic Njegos, Njegos`s birth house, Njegos`s Mausoleum on Lovcen, the court church Cipur, the Mausoleum of Bishop Danilo on Orlov krs and the Relief of Montenegro), the **Art Museum** with the Modern art gallery Dado Djuric, the **Ethnographic Museum**, and **Archaeological Museum with Lapidarium**. All of the museum units are located close to one another and they offer programs for visitors throughout the whole year.

Cetinje has a number of interesting places to see, explore and activities to do. Cultural institutions of both national and local importance are situated in Cetinje. The Ministry of Culture is located in this city, as well as the official residence of the President of Montenegro (**Blue Castle**), Royal National Theater "Zetski dom", **National Library**, **National Archive**, etc. Of particular interest for visitors is the **Vlach Church** (built in the 15th century) that has a yard fence made of pipe rifles that were confiscated in the liberation wars against the Ottoman Empire. The overall architecture of the city is attractive to tourists as well, especially the buildings of old embassies where now schools and universities are situated at. Cetinje is a small university city with numerous Art academies and residencies.

One of the most remarkable places is certainly **Njegos`s Mausoleum on Lovcen.** Beside of being a historical and cultural settlement, Mausoleum on Lovcen is well known for its magnificent landscape from which you can see almost the whole country. The Mausoleum is officially the highest located mausoleum in the World, as it is located in the height of 1660m (5450 ft). Locals will tell you that you haven't seen anything of Montenegro if you didn't visit Lovcen! On the way to Lovcen, you will find a beautiful natural residency **Ivanova Korita**, famous for its water source, sport, and recreational activities.

Cetinje is well known for the great food you can find at any corner, specifically national dishes, but also for its climate. It is one of the rainiest cities in Europe (around 4000 mm of rain a year), with dry and warm summers and mild and wet winters. Inhabitants of Cetinje are famous for their humor and extraordinary hospitality. In order to get a real picture of the whole country and meet Montenegrin history and culture – one definitely has to visit Cetinje.

Five kilometers away from Cetinje, visitors are pleased to see and visit one of the biggest surrender landmarks of the country – **Lipa Cave**. Lipa Cave was first opened more than 100 years ago (in 1918) but also closed for a long time. It was reopened in 2015 and it has numerous activities to offer: from train rides for kids, beautiful sightseeing, indoor and outdoor activities. Visiting Lipa Cave became an integral part of a visit to Cetinje. In addition to that, it is recommended to try traditional Montenegrin food in a nearby national restaurant Belvedere.

Must visit:

- **National Park Lovcen** (13 km from Cetinje)
- **National Museum of Montenegro** (all other cultural institutions are close to one another so it's easy to see them all)
- **Lipa Cave** (5 km from Cetinje), one of the biggest caves in ex-Yugoslavia with many interesting things to do. The place can be reached either by car or taxi (taxi from Cetinje will not cost more than a couple of euros).
- **Skadar Lake** and **Rijeka Crnojevica**, astonishing nature and attraction for hikers and bikers
- Try national and local dishes (Restaurant *Kole,*

Restaurant *Belvedere*). Make sure to try **njeguski prsut, njeguski sir and priganice**

Interesting facts:

Cetinje is called **Valley of Gods** (Dolina bogova), as there is an old legend by which God created Earth and only one place was left. Angels asked him about that territory and the God replied that this place will be home of Montenegrins and the country of Montenegro, while the place where he is standing now will be called Cetinje and each person that is born and raised there will be God.

Tips:

- Make sure to bring some warm clothes, no matter what time of the year you are visiting Cetinje and its surroundings. This is specifically important for those who are planning to visit Lovcen or even Lipa Cave.

Directions: Cetinje has a very convenient location as it is near Podgorica and Budva (two main cities of the country). Cetinje is accessible either by car or bus (30 minutes ride from Podgorica, 1-hour ride from Podgorica Airport, 20 minutes ride from Budva).

USEFUL INFORMATION:

- Cetinje bus station: (+382) 41 21 053
- National Museum of Montenegro: st. Novice Cerovića 7, (+382) 41 230 310
- National Park Lovcen, working hours: 9-17h

- Web: http://www.cetinje.me

PODGORICA

Podgorica is the capital city of Montenegro and its administrative, economic and business center. The city lies on five rivers (**Zeta**, **Moraca**, **Ribnica**, **Cijevna,** and **Sitnica**) and is located in the central region of the country. Podgorica is famous for its high temperatures during summer (above 40 degrees Celsius). Alongside with Madrid and Athens, it's one of the warmest cities in Europe. During winter, temperatures are also high and this is due to the effect that comes from the valley of river Bojana over Skadar Lake. Podgorica is, among all, a city with a long, rich and interesting history.

On the territory of contemporary Podgorica, Alta, Birziminium, and Doclea were three urban centers during Roman times. This place was inhabited by Slavs in the middle ages and named Ribnica. At that time, Podgorica was a lively center due to the high volume of trading and due to the routes that led to Trebinje and Dubrovnik. The development of the city stopped in the 15th century when the city was taken by the Ottoman Empire. In 1878 Podgorica was liberated by Montenegrins and it became the official part of the country, through the decision of Berlin Congress. During World War II, Podgorica was bombed and completely destroyed 72 times and was freed on 19th December 1944.

Podgorica might seem uninteresting to explore, as the city itself doesn't offer too much cultural and historical sites. This is due to the fact that Podgorica was completely demolished after WWII and it had to be rebuilt. The contemporary appearance of the city is a mix of communist architecture and modern high buildings.

Due to the destruction in World War II, very few cultural monuments remained in Podgorica: **Sahat-kula**, **Palace of King Nikola**, **Stara Varos** (Old town). The symbol of Podgorica is **Sahat-kula**, built in 18th century by Hadzi Pasa Osmanagic. It is located at the central Square Vojvoda Becir beg Osmanagic. Sahat-kula is 16m tall and once on its top was a clock that announced time every 30 minutes. The monument is protected by law and represents a significant part of Islamic presence on the territory of Podgorica and its history. **Stara Varos** is a neighborhood that originates from the Ottoman era. For 4 centuries, Stara Varos was the central part of Podgorica territory. Today, Stara Varos is attractive for visitors due to its specific architecture and winding streets. **The Palace of King Nikola** is placed in the heart of Podgorica and was built in 1891. At that time, the Palace served as a winter residence for King. The Palace of King Nikola, the Perjanic Home, the Palace Chapel, and the surrounding buildings were redecorated in the Art Gallery in 1984. Since 1985, it is a part of the Center for Contemporary Art and it hosts about 1500 works of art. Today, the Art Gallery in The Palace is one of the most eminent galleries in Montenegro.

Cultural life, additionally, is very rich in the capital of Montenegro. Significant cultural activities happen in Podgorica for the whole year. Most of the happenings are tied to the Palace of King Nikola, while city museums are constantly exhibiting collections of archeological sites but also of contemporary art. Association of writers of Montenegro is located in Podgorica, and all the biggest cultural manifestations are happening in this city, such as

International Book Fair, folk festivals, Podgorica Art Festival (PAF), Dzada Fest (Movie festival on the street), **Festival of International Alternative Theater** (FIAT), and many more. Three theaters can be found in Podgorica: **Montenegrin National Theater, City Theater,** and **Dodest**. Each of them offers a wide repertoire throughout the whole year, for both citizens and tourists. On the right bank of Ribnica, near the **City Museum**, there is a beautiful and colorful building, built in the 20th century, whose builder and the first owner was a well-known and popular doctor, dentist, Dr. Risto Kuslev. **Kuslev's house** was the place of the first dental school. Today there is a gallery space of the Public institution Museums and Galleries of Podgorica.

It's not surprising that Podgorica might seem slightly disappointing to the tourist – in terms of cultural and historical monuments. However, the city has to be respected as it developed largely after such a huge demolishing during the War. On the other side, Podgorica can offer a lot of activities and fun places for visitors, specifically when it comes to parties and nightlife. There is a whole street named **Bokeska ulica**, in the city center, with numerous cafes, pubs and night clubs that work seven days a week. Podgorica is well known for its nightlife, but also for a wide offer of restaurants and shopping places.

Even though Podgorica mostly consists of residential buildings, the city is full of green places, parks, hills. The main hill, after whom the city got its name, **Gorica** is a perfect place for any kind of activity (sport, recreation, walk...)

Surroundings of Podgorica hide rich archeological, historical and cultural treasures. Around 13km north-east from Podgorica, an old bridge **Medun** (Meteon) is located and it dates back from the ancient period. At first, Medun was a fortress and later on became a city. North of the upper city you will find a necropolis that dates from the Illyrian period.

The most important and impressive surrounding spot is certainly **Doclea** located between two rivers (Zeta and Moraca). Doclea was an ancient city with a population of around 10 thousand people. In the 1st century, Roman legions strengthened their power and Doclea became a political and cultural center of province Praevalitana. Doclea was almost completely destroyed in the 6th century when a catastrophic earthquake hit the place. Ruins of Doclea are open for visitors and they represent a valuable archeological spot.

Additional surrounding trips from Podgorica include a visit to **Eco-resort Plavnica, Mareza, Tuzi, Niagara Waterfalls, Skadar Lake, Kucka Korita, Bukumirsko jezero**.

Must visit:

- **Cathedral of Crist's Resurrection** (Saborni Hram Hristovog Vaskrsenja)
- **Sahat-kula** and **Old Town** (Stara Varos)
- **Doclea** ruins
- Eat at **Stara kuca, Restaurant Vuk**, Restaurant **Pod Volat**
- Take stunning photos at **Niagara Waterfalls** (there is also Niagara Restaurant).
- **Go-carting** (Karting Centar Podgorica).
- Visit **Adventure Pak Gorica**

Interesting facts:

During Yugoslavia, the city was named Titograd (after the President of Yugoslavia – Tito), and in 1992 it took back its old name, Podgorica.

Tips:

- Taxi ride through Podgorica usually costs around 1 euro, while the bus is 0.90€. Due to that, it is always more recommended to take a taxi through the city. An additional benefit is that taxi stations can be found in the whole city.

Directions: Podgorica is the capital of Montenegro and the city is well connected to most of European and World countries. The main Airport is located in Golubovci (13 km from the center of Podgorica). You can arrive in Podgorica also by bus, or train. Podgorica is well connected to each city in the country (by bus, train) but also to other regional countries.

USEFUL INFORMATION:

- Airport Podgorica: (+382) 20 444 233, info: +382 20 444 244,

web: http://www.montenegroairports.com

- Train station: (+382) 20 441 211/2; web: http://www.zcg-prevoz.me
- Bus station: (+382) 20 620 430; web: http://busterminal.me
- Hospital: (+382) 20 412 412
- Emergency: 124

- Police: 122

NIKSIC

Niksic is the second largest city in Montenegro located at a central-western part of the country. The city was built as early as in the 4th century by the Goths and its original name was Anagastum (later Onogost). The territory of Niksic has many parts originating from the Illyrian and Roman period and today they represent important cultural and historic monuments.

Niksic is an important industrial center of Montenegro, operating with a well-known **brewery Trebjesa**, bauxite deposits, forests, hydroelectric power station, etc. Besides being an industrial center, Niksic has a long tradition of being a central place for higher education. Additionally, the city is popular for its specific cultural scene that is concentrated mostly on rock and blues, alternative and underground art and culture. After World War I, Niksic also became an important cultural center, a place where lots of cultural activities were initiated (such as printing, literary magazines, and publishing, theaters, etc.).

Numerous cultural-historic sites and natural landscapes represent a high touristic potential of Niksic. The geographical position itself is very important as well: the city is located both near the capital city and near northern cities. Three rivers, three man-made lakes (**Slano Lake, Krupac Lake, Grahovsko Lake**) surrounded by high mountains are what makes Niksic an attractive destination and a breathtaking spot of nature. One of the most impressive spots is definitely **Tsar's bridge** (Carev most), located on the old road from Niksic to Trebinje (over Grahovo). It is one of the oldest Roman bridges in Montenegro, built with the help of Russian Tsar Alexander III, after whom it was named. In Niksic you will be able to find **Palace of King Nikola**, walls of city fortress **Bedem**, **Heritage Museum**, temples, and churches, but also many places to relax and enjoy nature.

Niksic is a vibrant city that gathers many artists, intellectuals, academics, and party people. Throughout the whole, city visitors will find places to enjoy, drink, have fun or party. Niksic is suitable for both summer and winter visits. In summer you can enjoy beautiful **Krupac Lake** with water sports and during winter **Vucje** ski center is the most attractive destination for winter sports and for enjoying winter moments. Park-forest **Trebjesa** is an attraction for both locals and visitors throughout the whole year. From the very top of Trebjesa, you can see the whole city. Trebjesa is one of the most famous Niksic picnic spots with lots of sport and recreational activities and tourist facilities. Lately, **Manitovac** became a breathtaking place for all visitors, especially for those traveling with family and children. Manitovac is only 1, 5 km away from the city center, located on the bank of the river Zeta. Cafe Park there offers a mini zoo, a children's playground, and beautiful breathtaking natural environment.

The surrounding of Niksic is especially important for local tourism, as it offers many beautiful sites and monuments. Among the most important is **Ostrog Monastery**, a miraculous place that people of all religions visit on a daily basis. Ostrog Monastery was built in the 17th century and it is definitely the most respected religious site. A lot of traditional customs are tied to Ostrog Monastery, such as walking to Monastery barefoot, leaving clothes or small money, lighting candles, buying holy water or icons.

High in mountains by Niksic, Monastery of Ostrog is found, the most respected religious site, built in XVII century. In it rest the remaining parts of St Vasilije Ostroski. There are Upper and Lower Monastery. In Lower konak is situated where pilgrims stay overnight in hope that St Vasilije Ostroski will help them.

Monastery Zupa is also close to Niksic, as well as a fortification **Susjed** from medieval ages. One of the most important prehistoric spots in the whole of Europe is located near Niksic (about 45 km away) and it's called **Red Rock** (Crvena stijena). This archeological spot has many cultural layers from various periods (Paleolithic, Mesolithic, Neolithic and Bronze age).

Each year, Niksic hosts two big rock festivals: **Lake fest** (on Krupac Lake) and **Bedem fest** (on Bedem fortress). These festivals are among most popular rock festivals in the region.

Must visit:

- Visit **Ostrog Monastery**. Directions: Main road Podgorica – Niksic, road Bogetici.
- **Park-forest Trebjesa**
- **Krupac Lake** (suitable for sports, fishing, many activities, and even enjoyable walk)
- **Manitovac** (parking available)
- Drink **Niksicko Beer**

Interesting facts:

Ostrog Monastery is well-known among people by its

miracles. A lot of people believe in the miraculous effect of this place and go to the Monastery to pray to St. Vasilije Ostroski, whose remaining are placed there. On the 12th of May, the day of St. Vasilije Ostroski, a lot of people from all around the World are part of a huge walk (pilgrimage). A special interesting fact is that people of all religions visit the Monastery on a daily basis and believe in miracles of St. Vasilije Ostroski.

Tips:

- Even though Niksicko Beer is good in all its sizes, shapes, and tastes, to get the real taste you need to try draught Niksicko Beer. You will find it in literally every café, pub, restaurant or club.

Directions: Niksic is easily accessible from all the parts of Montenegro. It's 55 km away from Podgorica and you can travel either by car, bus or train. Trains are available also from Bar. The city is well connected to the North of Montenegro, specifically Zabljak and Savnik. It takes an average 1-hour ride to the border with Bosnia and Herzegovina, and Niksic is well connected with Foca, Trebinje, and Sarajevo. Moreover, traveling from the seaside to Niksic is also easy as the detour Niksic – Trebinje leads to Risan in Boka Kotorska.

USEFUL INFORMATION:

- Train station: (+382) 40 214 480
- Bus station: (+382) 40 (+ 382)40 213 018
- Touristic Organization of Niksic: (+382) 40 212 511
- Ski center Vucje: 20 km from Niksic

- Police: 122
- Emergency room: 124

The northern region of Montenegro is ideal for nature lovers, lakes, rivers, mountain peaks, and active vacations. Good food is implied. Let's check!

INLAND MONTENEGRO

BERANE AND ANDRIJEVICA

Berane is geographically positioned at a very important place: it connects Montenegro with Serbia, Kosovo and Bosnia, and Herzegovina. Accordingly, many cultures passed through the region where Berane is incorporated at: from Illyrian, Celtic, Roman, Byzantine to Slavic, Ottoman, European and so on. The city got its name after Beran-village, a settlement near the city.

The territory of Berane was inhabited as early as in the Neolithic period and there are many traces of crossing of different cultures. Remains of material culture that can be found in Berane prove the presence of the Roman Empire. The remains of a military camp, **Roman Castrum**, from the Roman period can be found two kilometers from the city center. However, this territory was part of the Serbian kingdom until 1455 when the Ottoman Empire took over. The local population fought against the Ottoman Empire several times, but only in 1912 they managed to free their territory and from that time on the territory of Berane is an integral part of Montenegro.

The long Ottoman dominance left fingerprints in the architecture of the city, which is why the modern part of Berane has oriental lines. However, Berane is a center of Orthodox Christianity with many monasteries and churches. Among the most famous and important ones is certainly **Monastery Djurdjevi Stupovi**, built in the 12th century (1118). During the history, the Monastery played an important role in preserving national identity. It was attacked and demolished several times by Ottomans, and restored only in the 20th century. In addition to the Monastery Djurdjevi Stupovi, of great importance are monastery **Sudikova**, **Mosque in Harem**, and the **Temple of Saint Simeon Mirotocivi**. **Polimski Museum** in Berane has over 9000 exhibits of various interests, and those who are interested in history, archeology, art, and science are amused by the Museum work.

Berane can indeed offer numerous sports activities, due to the natural environment. Tourism in Berane is still not very much developed and tourists usually visit the city for one day or during the road trip to northern parts of the country. However, those who stay longer, usually stay at the famous **ski center Lokve** on Smilevica Mountain. Nature lovers can also visit the highest peak of the city which is called **Black head** (Crna glava) with 2 139m of height.

Touristic organization of Montenegro organizes annual winter sports festival named **Hot Winters in the Hills** (Vrela zima u Brdima) and it is located in Berane also. The Festival is a combination of sports and arts and it attracts professional athletes and artists of the whole region.

Andrijevica is a small beautiful city located in the north-east region of Montenegro. It has a population of only 5 071 people and the whole municipality territory is outspread on 263 km2. The city is surrounded by three high mountains: **Komovi**, **Bjelasica** and **Prokletije** and the place itself is one of the untouched diamonds of Montenegro. Andrijevica has a strong potential for mountain tourism and favorable conditions for ethnic tourism and visits.

The city got it's named after a church that was built by a certain Andrija. In the second half of the 19th century, Andrijevica was completely destroyed by the Ottoman Empire, but it recovered very soon and became a major political, cultural and economic center of Montenegrin tribe Vasojevici. Only after World War II, Andrijevica was incorporated to Ivangrad (now Berane), but it recuperated its municipality status again. Even though it's one of the smallest cities, Andrijevica has a vibrant cultural life that is centered mostly in the **Cultural Center of Andrijevica**.

Must visit:

- **Djurdjevi Stupovi Monastery**, **Jasikovac monument**, **Museum of Polimlje**
- **Ski center Lokve is** 15km away from the city
- Eat at **Restaurant Viaggio**, **Café Bistro** – the best cakes

Interesting facts:

Andrijevica is one of the youngest cities in Montenegro, founded in the 19th century.

TIPS:

- If visiting in winter, make sure to be part of Hot Winters in the Hills manifestation.

Directions: Berane is connected with other cities of Montenegro by two-laned motorways. It is well connected with Serbia, through Bijelo Polje (35 km away) or Rozaje. Berane can be reached by bus, almost from any city in the country. Most of the buses go from Podgorica, on an hourly basis. Berane used to have its own airport (Berane Airport) but it was closed and it is out of use. Podgorica Airport is 150 kilometers away.

USEFUL INFORMATION:

- Bus station Berane: (+382) 51 234 828
- Polimski museum: st. M. Malisica 2 (+382) 51 234 276
- Emergency room: 124
- Hospital (+382) 50 486 150
- Health center (+382) 50 432 722
- Police: 122

BIJELO POLJE

Bijelo Polje is one of the larger Montenegrin cities placed at the northern part of the country. The city has a rich cultural tradition and historical significance. Archaeological research showed the existence of a settlement in this region in the distant past. This region was inhabited even in the Neolithic period and had a turbulent history and a passing of different cultures. In the 12th century, the most important script was written in the Church of St. Peter in Bijelo Polje – *Miroslav Gospels*. ***Miroslav Gospels*** were written for Hum Prince Miroslav and today are kept in a National Museum in Belgrade.

Most of the cultural manifestations that are held in Bijelo Polje are organized by Cultural center Bijelo Polje and/or by the municipality. Those are **Festival of drama amateurs of Montenegro, Ratkovic's nights of poetry, International Tamburica orchestra festival, Bijelo Polje's painter's spring, Summer nights of music, Paint colony, Old bridge** etc. Alongside, in Bijelo Polje you will find a **Heritage Museum, Bijelo Polje Theater, Infobus (mobile library), Cinema, KUD Tekstilac, Literary club Miodrag Bulatovic, Library, Internet Center, cultural magazine Odzivi**. The most important monument in Bijelo Polje is **Church of St. Peter the Apostol**, built in the 13th century. The Church was a very important religious and cultural center from the very beginning. In the 17th century, during the Ottoman presence on this territory, they transformed the Church into the mosque. The Church regained its original role in 1912, after the liberation of Bijelo Polje from the Ottoman Empire, and was re-established in 1923. Even today, the Church of St. Peter the Apostol represents a significant monument of whole Montenegrin nation.

Bijelo Polje is very famous for numerous sports manifestations that are organized for the whole year. The most important ones are *Memorial indoor football tournament Momo, Saban, Vaso,* traditional volleyball tournament, basketball and paragliding cup in precise landing discipline, *memorial chess tournament Veselin Boskovic,* hill car race on track Sutivan - Jelah.

Great heritage treasure is located all in and around Bijelo Polje. Around 20km away from the city, and old bridge on river Bistrica made from stone in a crescent shape is located. A special attraction to both inhabitants and visitors is certainly river Lim – one of the longest rivers in Montenegro. Rafting on this river is a special adventure and suitable for everyone – for those who like peaceful enjoying in nature and for those seeking some adrenaline rush.

Around 25km away from Bijelo Polje, you will find amusing **Djalovica cave** (also called Cave above Devils upstream). This cave is located in the canyon of river Bistrica and on the left side of it is placed one of the smallest lakes – **Devil's upstream**. Only 16km of the cave have been explored to this day, while other parts remain unexplored. Thus, this place represents an attractive destination for both nature lovers and for archeologists and other scientists. An old bridge over Bistrica was built at the end of the 17th century and it is made of stones, while the form of a bridge is of a crescent moon. Visiting Bijelo Polje can't be full without visiting **Mountain Bjelasica** – a mountain that has a shape of a circle. The mountain Bjelasica is considered to be the most beautiful and the most majestic Montenegrin mountain. It is rich in running water and forest and has good potential for skiing. Its highest peak **The Black Head** is at 2139 meters above sea level, while its surface is about 630 square kilometers.

Bijelo Polje is also a treasurable place for mineral water with many sources (Banje Selo, Nedakusi, etc). The factory of Montenegrin **mineral water Rada** was found in Bijelo Polje in 1984. It stopped working for some time but is now reopened again. The specialty of this water is that it is drawn up from 6km underground. The name of the water comes after daisy flower – rada.

Must visit:

- **Church of St. Peter the Apostle**
- **Heritage Museum**
- **Djalovica Cave**

Interesting facts:

Church of St. Peter the Apostle in Bijelo Polje is included in the UNESCO list – Memory of the World and is represented as one of the most important movable monuments of the world's cultural heritage.

TIPS:

- Don't miss **cevapi Kod Senca** – the best cevapi in Montenegro. Open until 2:30 AM

Directions: The nearest airport is in Podgorica (130) km away, while the easiest transfer is either by bus or train. The main railway Bar – Belgrade passes through Bijelo Polje and it operates on a daily basis. Bijelo Polje is well connected to almost all cities in Montenegro by bus. Podgorica is 121km, Berane 37 km, Mojkovac 30 km, Kolasin 51 km, and Belgrade 350 km.

USEFUL INFORMATION:

- Train station: (+382) 50 478 560
- Bus station: (+382) 50 432 219
- Heritage Museum: Radnicka bb street, working hours: 08-16, entry fee: 1 euro, for children 0,5 euros
- Cultural Center V.B. Strunjo, Muniba Kucevica nr.17 (+382) 050/431-722,
- Hospital (+382) 50 486 150
- Emergency room 124
- Police 122
- Euro help 19812 (road assistance)

KOLASIN

In the high-mountainous part of northern Montenegro and on the right side of river Tara, a beautiful city and a ski paradise Kolasin is located. Kolasin is rather a small city, with no more than 8500 inhabitants. It is surrounded by mountains Sinjajevina, Semolja, Kape Moracke, Javorje, Magnik, Stravanj, and Ostrvice. A special diamond of this place are three canyons: **Canyons of Tara**, **Moraca,** and **Mrtvica**. The city was built in the 17th century by the Ottoman Empire. Their intention was to build a caravan station that will connect the coast and the north. Kolasin became part of Montenegro by the decision of Belin Congress. The tourist offer of Kolasin is enormous and very diverse and very convenient for both winter and summer tourism.

During summer, visitors can enjoy activities such **as hiking, cycling, horse riding, rafting or fishing**. The most famous hiking tour is to **Jablanov vrh**, which is the highest peak of mountain Sinjajevina. This place is the largest plateau in the whole Balkans, with the climb of around 1000 meters.

Kolasin territory is especially attractive for adventurers, as the city is surrounded by many hills and forests and represents a great opportunity for hikers.

Winter activities include a couple of **ski resorts, skiing, Nordic skiing, hiking, and other winter sports**. Kolasin is definitely a **ski paradise** with an average height of snow between 110 and 150 cm, while the highest point is over two meters. The average annual air temperature is 7.3°C, while the coldest month is January and warmest July. Some places in Kolasin (with the altitude higher than 1500m) are covered with snow for more than 120 days a year. One of the most famous and the best ski center of the whole region is located in Kolasin, **in Jezerina Kolasin Ski Center 1450**. Ski center is equipped with modern ski lifts, cable cars, restaurants, and a ski school. Kolasin Ski Center 1450 has 16.5 kilometers of arranged ski trails and they are classified and marked as light, medium heavy and heavy. This means that there are trails for all types of skiers and boarders from beginners to those most demanding and for those seeking adrenaline rush. The trails are prepared in the summer period so visitors can ski even when the height of the snow cover is minimal. Ski Center also has a system for artificial snowmaking at the foot of the ski slopes, which ensures that the ski season starts in mid-December and lasts until mid-April.

Kolasin is surrounded by many rivers and lakes, but also springs, streams, and wells. Caves such as **Cave Umovi** (at the altitude of 1945m), **Cave Vranstica** and **Cave Leura** are special attractions for both inhabitants and visitors. The city is surrounded by nine lakes, two rivers, many mountains, and canyons. Due to this, Kolasin is usually presented as an **air-spa** with natural richness.

One of the most valuable pearls in the European nature reserve is **Biogradska Gora**, not far from Kolasin. It is an area on a mountain massif rich in water surfaces and endemic plant and animal species, pastures, etc. Biogradska gora is under the strict protection of the state.

Botanical garden in Dulovina is filled with numerous vegetation samples and represents an important natural museum. In Botanical garden about 500 species can be seen, among them is a significant number of endemic species, and more than 80% are healing species. This unique botanical garden was founded in 1981 by Danijel Vincek. Vincek fell in love with Kolasin and its nature and decided to dedicate his life to the protection of the Montenegrin mountainous flora.

Kolasin is surrounded by bridges on river Tara also, while important architectural objects in the city are **Hunter's lodge** in Crkvine and **Memorial Home**. Kolasin's history is characterized by continuous battles and sufferings. An eternal struggle with Ottoman conquerors, the Balkan Wars, I and II World War. War and warfare are deeply imprinted not only in the memory of the Kolasin but also in the physiognomy of the city itself. Walking around Kolasin, you will find numerous monuments and features raised in memory of the liberation struggles of the people of this region. Most of them are from the Second World War when Kolasin was the war capital of Montenegro and the center of events crucial for the whole country.

In the Kolašin area, there are many important cultural and historical monuments, which have long found a significant place in history and cultural heritage. The most important of these monuments is certainly **Moraca Monastery**, which is located on the right bank of the river Moraca. The Monastery was built in the 13th century (in 1252). The

Moraca Monastery is fully painted and decorated with icons. Fresco, "The Raven feeds the prophet Elijah", created in the 13th century, is the oldest and most famous fresco of the Moraca Monastery.

Cultural life in Kolasin is supported by public cultural institutions, and most recently by a group named **Korifej Theater**. This group, with the support of Ministry of Culture, organizes **Internation Alternative Theater Festival Korifej**, each year from mid-July to mid-August. The Festival gathers many professionals and artists from all around the World and is one of the special diamonds of Montenegrin overall cultural scene. Kolasin has several cultural institutions, among most important ones, are **Cultural Center, Cinema, Library and Reading room, Heritage Museum, Cultural-artistic society Mijat Maskovic.**

Must visit:

- **Memorial Home**
- **Biogradska gora, Mountain Bjelasica, Village Crkvine, Moraca Monastery**
- Eat at **Restaurant Savrdak, Konoba,** or **Vodenica**

Interesting facts:

Biogradska Gora is one of the last three rainforests that are left in the whole of Europe.

Tips:

- Make sure to try Kolasin cheese called **kolasinski lisnati sir**. Goes great with **kacamak.**

Directions: Kolasin is accessible by train, bus or car. The nearest airport is in Podgorica (80 km) and Tivat Airport (154 km). The train that operates on the rail Bar – Belgrade stops at Kolasin and this is usually the easiest route (you can take the train at Bar, Podgorica, Niksic). The train station is 1.5 km away from the city center. Buses regularly go to Kolasin as the city is well connected to all other parts of Montenegro.

USEFUL INFORMATION:

- Train station: (+382) 20 441 492
- The cultural center, Heritage museum: Trg boraca 1, (+382) 20 Working hours 8 – 3
- Hospital: (+382) 20 865-140
- Emergency: 124

MOJKOVAC

Mojkovac is a small city, with a total area of 367 km2. It is located in the broadening of river Tara, between mountains Bjelasica and Sinjajevina and between National Park Biogradska gora and National Park Durmitor. Due to its convenient locations, Mojkovac is easily reachable and many tourists visit this city during their stay in the northern part of Montenegro.

Mojkovac was built in 13th century, during the reign of Serbian King Uros and the city was part of Serbian Kingdom of Raska. At that time, Mojkovac was the center of homonymous parish, mining, and trading, but also the center where Serbian silver coin was forged and made.

During Ottoman Empire, the first territory of Mojkovac that was freed was the one on the left side of river Tara (in 1878), and the territory on the right side of the river was freed only in 1912. Mojkovac became well-known city due to the Mojkovac battle that took place in 1916 during Orthodox Christmas. At that time, northern doors of Mojkovac and Montenegro were defended.

Visitors are amused by the **river Tara**, whose canyon is part of Durmitor national park (listed on UNESCO World Heritage list). Biogradska gora is located halfway between Mojkovac and Kolasin, and this Montenegrin diamond is also listed as National Park. Certainly, the biggest natural wealth of the municipality of Mojkovac is the most beautiful European river Tara, which the poets called "Tear of Europe". It is the longest Montenegrin river - 150 km, with clear and fresh water throughout the stream, rich in waterfalls and other natural phenomena. Its canyon is 78 km long and 1300 m deep, making it the most diving on our continent. At its rapids, the most spectacular competition and enjoyment of fast waters in the southern part of Europe are organized – rafting.

Mojkovac still didn't develop its full tourism potential, but it offers numerous activities, such as **paragliding, hiking, fishing, rafting, and kayaking**. Weather conditions in Mojkovac are ideal for paragliding throughout the year. Mojkovac, surrounded by mountains, is an ideal place for all possible winds. The Mojkovac paragliding club Phoenix, with the help of the Municipality, arranged many voyages on different locations. Anyone who wants to try to fly can do this with professional paraglide, in pairs, and the downhill will be safe. In the organization of the club Phoenix, in Mojkovac, the first competition was held - an individual inter-municipal paragliding championship. Paragliding in Mojkovac is a special attraction as nature around is wild and untouched and cannot be seen everywhere in the world.

Must visit:

- **Biogradska gora, Mountain Bjelasica**
- **Tara rafting**
- **Paragliding**

Interesting facts:

The legend tells that the name Mojkovac was formed by merging the word "moj kovani novac" (my coin money), which was pronounced by King Uros I while minting money at the Brskovo mine.

Tips:

- Don't miss eating at national restaurant **Kozak**. The restaurant is decorated in a traditional Montenegrin style (stone house) and offers a wide variety of national food prepared by traditional recipes. Extra tip: search for **kacamak**.

Directions: Mojkovac has a favorable traffic position. The possibilities of using the railway line Bar - Belgrade, the main road, Primorje - Podgorica - Belgrade, the regional road Mojkovac - Zabljak and Mojkovac - Pljevlja, as well as the proximity of the airports, represent good traffic communication with the surroundings. You can reach Mojkovac either by train, bus or car. Trains that operate on route Bar – Belgrade stops at Mojkovac and they operate on a daily basis. Mojkovac is easily accessible by buses, as the city is well connected with almost every city in the country.

USEFUL INFORMATION:

- Many agencies offer arrangements for rafting on Tara and visits to National parks
- Train station: (+382) 50 472 130
- Bus station +(382) 50 680 195
- Call code for Mojkovac: 050
- Police: 122
- Firefighters: 123
- Ambulance: 124
- Help on the road: 19807

PLAV AND GUSINJE

Plav is a small city in the north-eastern part of the Montenegrin mountains. It is located in the Plav-Gusinje valley. Plav got its name after Roman emperor Flavius (Phlavius) who was present in this region when the territory was under the Roman Empire. During history, Plav was an important crossroad that connected coast with Kosovo and Metohija and Albania. The Slavic tribes settled at this area at the end of the 6th and the beginning of the 7th century, pushing the Roman population out of the territory. Before the Ottoman conquest, Plav was a part of the Serbian Kingdom.

Many fortifications were built in this region during the middle ages. Most of them disappeared, while the most important ones are: **Plav's Didarev's city, Gusinje's city, Krsla, Jerin's city, Gradac,** and **Celigrad.**

Plav hides many cultural-historical monuments and those most important are: **Old Mosque in Plav, Church of St. Trinity in Brezojevici, Tower Redzepagica in Plav, Vizier's mosque in Gusinje** and ruined **Old bookshop** in Plav, which was built in 1471 by Plav beg Zejnel Dizdar.

Plav and its surroundings have a unique natural beauty, offering various activities for winter sports enthusiasts, as well as for those who like to enjoy beautiful waters of **Plav Lake**. This is the reason why this place is popular in ecological tourism - around Plav Lake there are eco-settlements and eco-hotels, where all the necessary conditions for relaxation can be found. In the winter you can find several ski centers on the slopes of Prokletije. Plav Lake is without a doubt the center of ecotourism in the region. Its clean water is ideal for swimming and in the winter it becomes a big skating rink. Competitions are held in navigation by boat, rowing, diving, and regatta. There are all conditions for sports fishing. It is believed that water from the lake has medicinal properties.

National Park Prokletije is a place of great significance. It gained the status of a national park in 2009 and attracts tourists from all over Europe with its high slopes (over 2000 m) and a large number of glacier lakes - there are 6 in the park. In the national park, you will find three different climatic zones. This is a unique national reserve with a wide variety of flora and fauna.

Even though a small city, Plav is a host of many cultural manifestations, such as **Days of blueberry, Sculpture and art colony, Literary meetings, Festival of folk music: Singing youth**.

Gusinje is placed right next to the Albanian border. There is not much information about Gusinje from the earlier centuries. The story says that in the 14th century there was a village Gusino in this area which today might be municipality Gusinje.

Must visit:

- **Alipasini izvori**
- **Visitorsko Lake**
- **Vizier's Mosque**
- **Redzepagica Tower**
- **Church of St. Trinity**
- **National Park Prokletije**
- **Plav Lake**

Interesting facts:

Plav Lake is the second largest lake on the territory of ex-Yugoslavia.

Tips:

- Make sure to visit Plav during the manifestation Days of blueberries. This manifestation is held every year, starting from 2000.

Directions: You can reach Plav and Gusinje by buses from Podgorica, Niksic or some of the northern cities.

USEFUL INFORMATION:

- Bus station: (+382) 51 251 371
- Emergency room: 124
- Police: 122

PLJEVLJA

Pljevlja is one of the largest cities in Montenegro, located in the north-western part of Montenegro. It lies in the middle of Pljevlja valley and valley of river Cehotina. The name of Pljevlja was first mentioned in the 15th century, but when Ottoman Empire took over the place, they changed the name into Taslidza (Stoney place), which was only a temporary name. Pljevlja recovered its independence and became an integral part of Montenegro and a symbol of the meeting point of Christianity and Islam.

During the Middle Ages, Pljevlja was a city-railroad, a place of meeting of culture. This is where trade caravans from the west to the mighty Constantinople passed, and from that time on, Pljevlja is considered the point of connecting Christianity and Islam. During this period, the most beautiful monuments of these two religions in the area of Southeast Europe were built, which consist of symbols of the city and the seal of eternal tolerance, coexistence, multi-ethnicity, culture and represent architectural sights - the **Monastery of Holy Trinity** and the **Husein Pasa Mosque**.

These two monuments remain until today and represent a treasurable sign of mutual respect and equality.

The city of Pljevlja is surrounded by mountain massifs and hills, while three rivers flow through the city: **Breznici, Cehotina,** and **Vezisnici**.

Pljevlja is an important cultural and historical place. During history, the city served as a road that led to Constantinople, but it was also a center of exploiting zinc, lead, mercury, ores, etc. Pljevlja is especially interesting for archeologists and for those who love archeological spots, as 3 km south-west from Pljevlja you can find archeological digs of **Roman city Municipium S**. At about 20 km from Pljevlja there are remains of another city, **Koznik**, which once served as a protection of mines of lead and zinc. **Heritage Museum** in Pljevlja keeps important materials and also has a significant role in the cultural development of the whole city.

Husein Pasa's mosque is one of the most significant spots for Muslims in the whole Balkan region. The Minaret itself is 42 meters tall and it has several domes. Inside Husein Pasa's mosque are kept some of the most beautiful Islamic books and writings, as well as Quran script from the 16th century.

The Monastery of St. Trinity is located 1.5. km away of Pljevlja and the place represents an important Orthodox temple. It was built on the remains of a monastery that dates back in the era of Nemanjici. The library of the Monastery keeps important and valuable scripts, from the 12th and 14th century.

City Park Vodice is one of the most attractive places in the whole city. As the legend says, it was a former estate of the Holy Trinity Monastery. The park is surrounded by beautiful forests and decorated with walking paths. City Park is divided into two parts of river Breznica. At this point, two artificial lakes can be found.

Must visit:

- **Ali-Pasa's Mosque, Monastery of St. Trinity**
- **Heritage Museum**

Interesting facts:

Surroundings of Pljevlja hide many amazing excursion spots, such as Rudnica, Zeleni Vir, Mejtef, Perova luka, Krakalice, Meandri Cehotine, etc.

Tips:

- Visit City Park Vodice for a night walk! Most of the locals walk during the night through this park and it's a very vibrant and lively place.

Directions: The easiest way to reach Pljevlja is by bus. Daily bus departures from Podgorica, Niksic, Bar, Herceg Novi (main road through Budva), Sarajevo, Belgrade, Novi Sad. The city, due to its location, is well connected not only with Montenegrin cities but also with the whole region (Serbia, Bosnia and Herzegovina, Kosovo). The nearest train station is located in Bijelo Polje, at a distance of 82 km from Pljevlja. Pljevlja can be reached by train from Prijepolje (Serbia) as well, at a distance of 36 km. Podgorica Airport is 178 km away, Tivat Airport 233, while the nearer airport is in Sarajevo (148 km).

. . .

USEFUL INFORMATION:

- Bus station: (+382) 52 323 114
- Heritage Museum: Trg 13. jul bb, (+382) 52 322 002;
- Monastery of St. Trinity: 1,5 km away from Pljevlja, visits are arranged by appointment
- Husein-Pasa's mosque: Ul. Vuka Knezevica 4, visits are arranged by appointment
- Police: 122
- Firefighters: 123
- Emergency: 124

PLUZINE

The Municipality of Pluzine is by the size of the seventh biggest municipality in Montenegro. The municipality is located in the north-west of Montenegro, along with the border of Bosnia and Herzegovina. Historically. It is an old-age region and is located in the central parts of so-called Stara Hercegovina. Pluzine were incorporated to Montenegro after the Berlin Congress in 1878. In the narrower, regional sense, the municipality can be classified as a part of the extensive Durmitor region belonging to the municipalities of Plužine, Savnik, and Žabljak.

Historically, the Piva area was inhabited in prehistoric times. Archaeological research in the **cave Odmut** then, eight cultural layers and large amounts of coal, ash, and fire, crusting stone and clay vessels have been discovered. Bones and deer horns with well-preserved traces of artistic design have been found.

The city is most famous for its astonishing and untouched

wild beauty. The whole city is surrounded by mesmerizing nature. Forests, mountain pastures, and beauty of Durmitor, Maglic, Volujak and other mountains, ice lakes Trnovačko, Stabanjska, Veliko and Malo Škrčko are exceptional natural beauties for visiting and developing tourism. Tourists usually visit Pluzine as a day trip, during their stay in northern parts of Montenegro. Not to miss is an excursion on **Piva Lake, canyon Susice, Nevidio, Trnovacko lake, and Piva Monastery**.

The tourism in Pluzine developed largely after the establishment of **Nature Park Piva** that offers a wide variety of activities, natural sightseeing spots, ethno villages, etc. Park Piva connects two National parks (Durmitor and Sutjeska in Bosnia and Herzegovina). The place is rich with versatile relief, mountainous landscapes, forests, canyons of Tara, Piva and Susica, mountain lakes, etc. This place is a little piece of heaven on Earth, worth visiting at least once!

The ideal conditions for hunting, fishing, rafting Tara, Piva lake cruises, hiking and mountain biking are just a part of what this region has to offer to tourists. In addition, a hidden gem of this area is definitely ethno villages, where the World completely stops for a moment.

Must visit:

- **Nature Park Piva**
- **Piva Monastery**
- **Piva Lake**

Interesting facts:

Even though Pluzine is a large municipality, it has a total population of only 3246 inhabitants.

Tips:

- If visiting Park Piva, make sure to stay in one of the bungalows, built on traditional appearance.

Directions: You can reach Pluzine by bus or car. Buses go from Podgorica (109 km) and Niksic (58 km). The city is very close to the border with Bosnia and Herzegovina.

USEFUL INFORMATION:

- Park Piva website: https://www.parkpiva.com/

ROZAJE

Rozaje is located at the end of the north-eastern part of Montenegro. The city is surrounded by marvelous mountains, forests, and rivers. The population in Rozaje mostly consists of Muslims (95%) of Montenegrin, Bosnian and Albanian nationality. The territory of the municipality of Rožaje belongs to the best-preserved environments in Montenegro and has exceptional tourist potentials. Rarely inhabited mountain and cattle areas abound in green landscapes: forests, pastures, and healthy mountain climate, clear springs, beautiful river valleys, the magnificent canyon of river Ibar, attractive cattle houses and excellent ski fields covered with snow for several months.

Rozaje villages and surroundings are oases of peace,

tranquility and untouched nature. This area is a great combination of rural and ecological tourism with the main offer of preserved nature, traditional rural hospitality, and healthy food. Offer is very diverse: from mountaineering hike, alpinism, cycling, jeep photo safari, hiking, and biking.

Besides being a place of natural wonder, Rozaje is rich with **national tradition** (folklore, anecdotes, folk poetry, etc.).

Many monuments from Middle ages to the Ottoman Empire can be found on the territory of Rozaje. Some of the most important are: **Church Ruzina in Suhi Dol**, **Church Gospodjin vrh** at the homonymous mountain, **Kurtagic mosque** which was built in 1698 by Sultan Murat II, **Kucanska mosque** built in 1839, **Ganica Kula** built in first years of XIX century.

Cultural life in Rozaje is mostly led by the **Cultural Center of the City**. Manifestations and activities, such as **Festival of Children's songs Golden Snowflake** (Zlatna pahulja), **Hot winter in the hills** (Vrela zima u brdima) are organized annually. Cultural Center is in charge of the organization of cultural life and manifestations. Center, among other things, publishes a magazine **Rozaje's collection (Rozajski zbornik)** organizes promotions of books, art exhibitions and especially exhibitions of homeland painters gathered in association **Kula**.

River Ibar flows through the city, while its canyon is almost impassable and represents one of the rare natural untouched treasures.

Must visit:

- **Ganica Kula**

- **Hiking and biking**
- **Kucanska Mosque**
- **Church Ruzina**

Interesting facts:

Rozaje is one of the rare cities in Montenegro in which women are covered in hijabs. Thus, be sure to dress and act modestly.

Tips:

- Make sure to try a local dish called **jardum**. It's a sheep's milk that has to be salted and flavored then cooked in a low-melting flask with constant stirring, while the whole surface is not covered with foam. Then the vessel is removed from the fire to cool down. This milk, when it cools, is very dense and tasty. Usually, it is served at the end of the meal.

Directions: You can reach Rozaje by bus or car. Most buses go from Podgorica, Niksic or other northern cities (Bijelo Polje or Mojkovac). Rozaje can be reached from three sides: road Bijelo Polje – Berane, Novi Pazar – Kosovska Mitrovica, the road that connects Kosovo and Macedonia.

USEFUL INFORMATION:

- Heritage Museum Ganića kula: st. Devete crnogorske brigade bb, by appointment, (+382) 67 503 915

ZABLJAK AND SAVNIK

At the base of mountain **Durmitor**, you will find a lovely city of Zabljak. The city is considered to be the highest populated settlement in south-east Europe. The altitude of 1450 meters makes this city the highest urban settlement in the whole Balkans. The story says that this city was first called Varezina Voda and Anovi (Hanovi) but that it was renamed to Zabljak after frogs (Montenegrin: zaba) from Otoke region, who would croak every year in the wake of spring, and announce its arrival.

Durmitor is the biggest attraction in this area. With its exceptional natural beauty, specific hydrography, a special relief, as well as a very rich and interesting living world, the mountain massif of Durmitor deserved to be proclaimed National Park in 1952. Located in the northwest of Montenegro, the park includes the main Durmitor massif with the Tara canyon, Draga and Sušica canyon and upper part of the Komarnica canyon valley, covering an area of 39,000 ha. Durmitor National Park abounds with a significant number of cultural monuments from the ancient period to the modern age. The most impressive are medieval monuments: the ruins of cities and fortifications, bridges and shops, necropolises and monastery complexes in the valley of the Tara River. The highest peak of Durmitor is **Bobotov kuk** (2523), while Durmitor is one of the highest mountains in Dinarides. Durmitor is filled with 18 lakes, while the largest one, **Black Lake** (Crno jezero), is a real diamond of nature. The Black Lake is made of two Lakes: Big (Velje) and Small (Malo). Zabljak is a very famous ski destination, but this area can offer other activities, such as hiking, rafting, jeep safari, biking, etc.

For lovers of extreme sports and adventure, the **Nevidio canyon** of the river Komarnica river will be a good opportunity to enjoy. What is characteristic of the Nevidio

Canyon is the fact that a smaller number of people have seen it than Mount Everest, because it is quite inaccessible, and in the poached parts it is only 40cm to 1 meter wide.

Opposite to Durmitor is the hill **Pirlitor** where the remains of the medieval city can be found. According to the legends, this place was the seat of Durmitor Duke Momcilo. Durmitor is attractive also because it is the home of many rare animals, such as chamois, eagles, hawks, grouse, bears, wolves and the territory has around 130 species of different birds. More than 1500 plant species live on this area, and most of them are rare and endemic kinds.

Durmitor region is recognizable by **culinary specialties**. The local food is mostly made of dairy and meat products. Here you will try the best Montenegrin cheese and scrap, grits and well-known **kackavalj**. Zabljak is very famous for its lamb dishes as well.

The municipality of Zabljak organizes many manifestations, and most of them are tied to traditional and rural customs. Zabljak is, however, a very popular destination for New Year's celebration, with many cafes and pubs organizing parties.

Savnik is the smallest municipality in Montenegro with a population of only 2070 people. Savnik was founded in the second half od 19th century (1861) by traders. Savnik is a city with 5 rivers and many natural landmarks. The city is usually connected with Zabljak, as they are really near.

Savnik is known for two natural phenomenon's, here during the days around the equinox sun rises and sets twice. The second one appears in summer in draught time on river Savnik, which in a few hours completely dries and then comes flowing again.

. . .

Must visit:

- **National par Durmitor**
- **Bobotov kuk**
- **Zminje Lake**
- **Greek necropolis**
- **Nevidio Canyon**

Interesting facts:

The hiking tradition in Durmitor has existed **for more than one century**. In this region with extreme climatic conditions and great natural potentials, hiking is the first in a series of activities that Durmitor offers to its guests. Whether you are interested in alpinism, running, sport climbing, free climbing, or just the excursion, Durmitor will amaze you. Make sure not to go alone on some tours, as nature can be tricky sometimes and strangers can get lost.

Tips:

- Buy homemade honey and berries, as this region is famous for it.

Directions: From Podgorica to Zabljak you can take a bus, especially if you do not know Montenegrin roads. Departures are from the Podgorica bus station and take about 2:30 to 3 hours. You can also go with your own car, or rent-a-car, so you will come from Podgorica via Kolasin to Mojkovac, then turn from the main road leading to Serbia towards Zabljak. You can also go from Niksic and Savnik from Podgorica and in a couple of hours, you will find yourself in Zabljak. Zabljak is very easy to reach, as this is a popular destination for tourists, and the roads that lead to the city are all marked.

USEFUL INFORMATION:

- Touristic Organization of Zabljak: (+382) 52 361 802
- National park Durmitor: Visitor center: tel: (+382) 52 36 02 28

NATIONAL PARKS

CONSIDERING THE SIZE OF THE WHOLE COUNTRY, Montenegro is one of the rare small countries with 5 National parks: **NP Durmitor (1952), NP Biogradska Gora (1952), NP Lovcen (1951), NP Skadarsko jezero (1983)** and **NP Prokletije (2009)**. Each National park is a special piece of beauty for itself and visiting all of them is a treasurable experience.

National Park Durmitor covers the area of **Zabljak municipality, Savnik, Pluzine, Pljevlja, and Mojkovac** and it belongs to the northwestern part of the country. The total surface is 39000 ha, and elevation is between 500 to 2525m at the highest peak – **Bobotov kuk**. However, the most popular and most visited peak of the National Park Durmitor is **Savin Kuk**. Its eastern slope can be reached by a chairlift, several hundred meters below the highest point, near Savina Voda. The chairlift belongs to the Ski Center Durmitor and significantly helps to get to know the beauty of the eastern part of Savin Kuk, which rises 800 meters above Jezerska Visoravna. This side of the Durmitor is called the Clean Side. The snow cover at Durmitor is held 120 days a year, and the best ski slopes are on the slopes of Savin Kuk, Stuoca and Javorovace.

Durmitor is rich with more than 18 frosty lakes which are called **Eyes of the Mountain**. The most beautiful and most attractive lake is **Black Lake** (Zabljak municipality). The name of this lake came from the reflection of the tall coniferous forests that surround it. The Peak that rises above Black Lake is called **Medjed** (Bear).

Along the **canyon of the river Tara**, which is the deepest cliff of Europe, dense pine forests are sprinkled with clear lakes, which are home of a large number of endemic plants. This canyon was also proclaimed as a World Ecological Reserve. The whole Durmitor territory is rich with vegetation and various endemic and relict species. Alongside with that, this area has a wide social legacy: from necropolis, Greek and Roman graveyards, to churches and monasteries, etc. UNESCO listed Durmitor on its World Heritage List in 1980.

Opportunities for visitors are very wide, with a lot of attractions and fun activities. Starting from going through the most profound canyon in Europe (Canyon Tara) and swimming in flawlessly clean water to jeep safari, hiking, biking, climbing, and horse riding. Most of the tourists (and usually those traveling with families) chose to explore this park by bike which can be rented. National Park Durmitor is an attraction during both summer and winter and has an offer for each period of the year. Either you want to enjoy skiing and winter holidays or get away from hot weather – National Park Durmitor will know how to host you. This place is attractive for anyone: hikers and adventurers, families, couples, sports teams, athletes, individuals, friends.

USEFUL INFORMATION:

- Phone: (+382) 52 36 02 28
- E-mail: npdurmitor@nparkovi.me
- Ticket (including visits to the Visitor Center, educational trails): 3,00 € (except for children up to 7 years)
- Ticket for organized groups of pupils, students, pensioners, trade union organizations and mountaineering organizations (including a visit to the Visitor Center and Educational Paths) - with a written request and approval from the Park Director 1,50 €
- Ticket for the Visitor Center € 1.00
- Ticket for 3 days 6,00 €; Ticket for 7 days 12,00 €
- Rent a boat on Black Lake 8,00 € for 1 hour
- Rent a bike 3,00 € for 1 hour and 8,00 € for the whole day
- Camping: Use of space for setting up a tent 3,00 € a day; Caravan 3,00 € a day
- Kayak tours price ranges between 20 to 70 euros and it depends on the route one is planning to do

National Park Lovcen is located in the Central region and it covers the territory of Cetinje. The total surface is 6220 ha, while the elevation ranges between 939 to 1769m. The highest peaks are Sinovnik (1,749 m) and Jezerski vrh (1,657 m)

Each Montenegrin will immediately tell you that Lovcen is the **symbol of Montenegro**, and, moreover, a part of national identity and personality. The seven rulers of the **Petrović dynasty** come from the famous tribe Njegusi. During their 200 years rule (from the 17th to the beginning of the 20th, they left a strong stamp on cultural and historical circumstances in Montenegro.

Many natural and cultural-historical spots are what makes Lovcen famous and recognizable throughout the whole World. Among the 1,300 plant species, which makes 1/3 of the total Montenegrin flora, there are many endemic, relict, medicinal, aromatic and honeycombs species. The park area is a habitat of many animal species, with numerous endemic and relic forms. Apart from mammals (wolf, bear, fox, deer, rabbit, hedgehog, Montenegrin voles, etc.), there are numerous other animal groups, about 200 species of birds, 11 species of reptiles, 5 species of amphibians, 85 species of butterflies, 100 species of ants, 45 species of flies, 10 species of sunbathers, etc. Development of a few kinds of vegetation and numerous greeneries on Lovcen were affected by the topographical position of the place and the juncture of two climatic zones (Mediterranean and continental). The place is attractive to visitors during both summer and winter season.

The cultural and historical values of Lovćen are characterized by a diverse architectural heritage - memorial complexes, sacred and profane rural architecture and technical facilities, concentrated on the wider area of Njegusi and Ivanova Korita. In addition to that, in Lovcen you will find numerous churches of simple architecture, as well as traditional buildings (stone houses centuries old). In Njegusi (small village Erakovici), you will find the memorial house of the Montenegrin rulers of the Petrović dynasty, and at the top of Lovcen (Jezerski vrh), you will see the grandiose

Mausoleum of the Montenegrin lord, the famous poet, and bishop **Petar II Petrović Njegoš.**

There are many activities visitors can enjoy during their stay at National Park Lovcen: from visiting Ivanova Korita resort to Adventure Park. **Walking tours** on Lovcen are very attractive to both inhabitants and tourists. There are three main walking paths, very developed, and their length varies from 4,5 km to 13 km. **The Adventure Park** is located on Ivanova korita and it covers the area of 2 ha. It has 10 tracks and offers a wide range of opportunities for sports and extreme adrenaline activities. Each track in the Adventure Park has about 15 different games that are located at certain heights, and are specially adapted for the age of 5 to 70 years. Each user of the park receives the necessary equipment (belt, helmet, gloves), and there is an expertly trained team of instructors who will explain to each user how to use and apply all the games and activities.

The best place to try typical Montenegrin food, each inhabitant is very proud of, is definitely Lovcen. There you will find famous **njeguska prusta** (smoked ham) and **njeguski sir** (cheese). Also, do not hesitate to try **priganice** and other typical Montenegrin dishes. The special taste and aroma of these specialties, which are precisely characteristic for this area, is conditioned by the mixing of mountain and sea air, as well as the wood used for drying them. For this reason, the entire area of Lovcen is famous for the drying of meat. Food from this area is very famous and people still talk about an interesting story of a visit from a famous writer - George Bernard Shaw. During his visit to Montenegro, Bernard Shaw visited Lovcen as well. Locals wanted to host him generously and welcome him in the best manner, so they prepared numerous dishes and typical food. However,

Bernard Shaw didn't express any emotion and asked for a potage. A lady brought him a dish that now has a name „Ono" (That) and the famous writer was so impressed that he took a notebook to write down the recipe. A lady cook said that he can't write the recipe because he would have to take the whole Lovcen area to his home in order to make this dish. Thus, the authenticity of Lovcen food is very famous throughout the whole World and visiting this area can't be a full enjoyment without trying at least one food specialty.

USEFUL INFORMATION:

- Entrance Fee (including visits to the Visitor Center, Educational Trails): 2,00 € (except for children up to 7 years)
- Ticket for organized groups of students, students, pensioners, trade union organizations and hiking associations (including visits to the Visitor Center, educational paths) - with a written request and approval from the Park Director 1,50 €
- Bike rental 2,00 € for one hour and 8,00 € for the whole day
- Use of guide services 60 € for 4 hours and 100 € for 8 hours
- Accommodation (bungalow) 30,00 € for one day
- Camping: Use of space for setting up a tent 3,00 € a day; Camping trailer 10,00 € / day
- All information regarding National Park Lovcen visitors can get at Visitor center

National Park Biogradska gora covers the area of the municipality of Berane, Andrijevica, Kolasin, and Mojkovac, between rives Tara and Lim, and at the central part of mountain Bjelasica. Its total surface is around 5650 ha and is situated at an elevation of 832 m. Even though Biogradska gora holds the status of a National Park from 1952, even in 1872 Montenegrin King Nikola I secured this area by law and evaluated the natural legacy. National Park Biogradska gora is the first National Park in Montenegro, but also one of the first in the World, as it was put under the protection of the state as early as in 19th century.

There are four types of climate that collide in this area: moderate continental, Mediterranean, sub-mountainous and mountainous. Tourists who want to escape hot summers can visit National Park Biogradska gora, as the average summer temperature is around 17 ° C. During winter, this area is attractive for snow lovers, as the snow on Bjelasica lasts up to 120 days a year. **Mountain Bjelasica** is considered to be one of the greenest mountains in the whole country.

Visitors come to National Park Biogradska gora primarily to see the **rainforest**, one of the last three rainforests left in Europe. Some parts of the rainforest are used for scientific research. A special diamonds of National Park Biogradska gora are its unique ice lakes: **Biogradsko Lake, Pesica Lake, Usulovacka Lakes,** and **Sisko Lake**. The biggest one is **Biogradsko Lake**, located at an altitude of 1094 meters. At this place glacier melted in the past and created a water surface. The deepest point of Biogradsko Lake is 12, 1 meter.

The highest peak of National Park Biogradska gora is called **Black Head** (Crna glava), located 2139 meters above sea level. Other famous peaks are Troglava and Zekova glava.

This area is rich in nature with numerous endemic species, vegetation, greeneries, animals. There are 26 separate plant communities in the Park, with about 2,000 plant species and about 90 species of trees. An animal world is rich with 200 species of birds, 80 species of butterflies, 350 species of insects and typical mammals (wolf, bear, fox, deer, squirrel, fallow). In the forests of Biogradska gora there are trees which are 400 years old. Due to its clean air and healthy environment, National Park Biogradska gora is considered to be an air spa.

Activities in National Park Biogradska Gora are wide: from hiking, riding, biking, skiing in winter, snowboarding, to walking tours. Walking paths are well marked and the tours can be organized with the help of professional guides. Those who want to have a larger view on the National Park can climb the 26 meters high observation post and enjoy the beautiful scenery. In the National Park, you will also find the so-called Education Trail, where you can get all the information about rich flora and fauna of this area.

Biogradska gora, as well as the surroundings, had a turbulent history, so this place is an important archeological spot as well. Visitors are able to see remains of waterfalls, towers, log cabins, and similar objects, and hear stories from some very old times.

This area is famous for the best **kacamak** and **cicvara** – two important Montenegrin national dishes. Traditional dishes of mountain areas of Bjelasica and Sinjajevina are conditioned by the richness of pasture, so the food is mostly made up of dairy products and meat. Another specialty of this area is the lamb meat, cooked and baked under the bush, which only has a specific and recognizable taste here.

National Park Biogradska gora is easily accessible from Podgorica or northern cities, by bus, train or car.

USEFUL INFORMATION:

- Entrance fee for National Park Biogradska gora (including visits to the Visitor Center, educational trails): 3,00 € (except for children up to 7 years)
- Ticket for organized groups of pupils, students, pensioners, trade union organizations and hiking associations (including visits to the Visitor Center, educational trails) - with a written request and the approval of the Park Director € 1.50
- Rental of boats on Biogradsko Lake 8,00 € for 1h
- Use of guide services € 60.00 for 4 hours and 100,00 € for 8 hours
- Bike Rental 3,00 € for 1 hour and 10,00 € for the whole day
- Kayaking rental (one-seat) 3,00 € for 1 h; Rental of kayak (two-seat) € 5.00 for 1 h
- Accommodation (bungalow) - per person 10,00 € / day
- Camping: Use of space for setting up a tent 3,00 € a day; Camping trailer 10,00 € / day

National Park Skadar Lake is located at the south-central part of the country and it covers the municipalities of **Podgorica, Bar**, and **Cetinje**. It's one of the most famous National Parks of Montenegro and of the most famous landmarks of the whole country. The National Park Skadar Lake has the surface of 40 000 ha and is situated at an elevation of 5 m. The climate is sub-Mediterranean, with mild and rainy winters (the lowest monthly average water temperature in January is 7.3 ° C). The summers are dry and hot with maximum air temperature above 40 ° C and a water temperature above 27 ° C. The average air temperature is 14.9 ° C.

Skadar Lake is the biggest lake in the whole Balkans (43 km long and 13 km wide) and is the home of many endangered species. This is the only National Park dominated by aquatic and wetland ecosystems, and the long northern coast developed ideal conditions for the living world, specifically bird life. The greatest winged animal in Europe, **pelican**, lives on Skadar Lake. There are 281 species of birds on the Lake, nesting, wintering or moving, so the Lake has the status of the Area of International Importance for Bird Living and is on the world list of aquatic habitats of international importance. One of the reasons that Skadar Lake is called a "paradise for birds" is that various species of ducks can also be found in its area, but also goose. There are 48 species of fish in the park, 50 species of mammals, numerous amphibians, reptiles, and insects.

Skadar Lake has a rich history and culture, and, thus, numerous archaeological sites, medieval monasteries and churches, fortifications and folk architecture (fishing villages, old bridges, mills, and wells). Specific national architecture - old rural units, individual examples of fishing and residential buildings, stone bridges and mills on river watercourses, confirm the cultural landscape of a particular architectural value. This diverse and rich cultural and historical heritage also proves that Skadar Lake was an important historical, economic and cultural center in the past. From the numerous archaeological sites, the most interesting ones are from the Illyrian-Hellenistic and Roman periods, and several spots of medieval sacral architecture. The most significant and most representative cultural and historical value of the National Park Skadar Lake consists of monasteries from the 14th and 15th centuries from the time of the rule of Balsic and Crnojevic dynasties and fortification complexes from the period of Ottoman domination. A significant legacy of the Skadar Lake relates to cultural goods such as archaeological finds, manuscripts, icons in permanent museum settings.

Activities for visitors are wide: fishing, birdwatching, cycling, cruising, walking tours. Cruising around the Skadar Lake is a full enjoyment of the natural beauties, numerous islands, hills, cultural and historical monuments. Beautiful, hidden beaches and bathing in the Lake are an integral part of this adventure. The tourist offer also includes traditional wooden boats - chunks. Cruising around the Lake is done in the organization of licensed professionals. The ships depart from the ports in Vranjina, Virpazar, and Plavnica. Numerous manifestations are held every year on this area, such as: **Skadar Lake Trophy** (July 13), **Festival of Wines and Bans** (second half of December), **Festival of Nature and Culture** (September), **Kostanijada** (end of October, beginning of November), **The day of ecology, tourism, culture and sports** (during the summer months)

The traditional cuisine of this area is mostly fish, specifically crap in the pan and an eel prepared on a bowl of rice or baked on a spit. Most of the fish that is caught is dried in smoke. At the table, along with the perfectly prepared fish, you will be able to find the wine that represents the traditional product of this region. **Crmnica** is a cradle of autochthonous vine varieties of the spleen and a short stint. This area was for centuries home of wines and winemaking and the products made here are well-known in the whole

World. The food offer in the area of Skadar Lake is rich with cheese, olives, olive oil, and wine.

The National Park Skadar Lake can be approached from 3 different sides (Podgorica, Cetinje, and Bar) and each side has its own unique beauty. The train that goes from Bar to Podgorica stops at a small village **Virpazar**.

USEFUL INFORMATION:

- NP Skadar Lake Prices The venue (including a visit to the Visitor Center in Vranjina and Virpazar, the theme center in Rijeka Crnojevića, educational trails, as well as the use of the observation platform for birds): 4,00 € (except for children up to 7 years)
- Ticket for organized groups of students, students, pensioners, trade union organizations and hiking associations (including visiting the Visitor Center in Vranjina and Virpazar and the thematic center in Rijeka Crnojevića, educational paths) - with a written request and approval from the Director of the Park 2,00 €
- Ticket for 3 days 8,00 €
- Ticket for the Visitors Center of the National Parks - Vranjina 2,00 €
- Thematic center and educational path - Rijeka Crnojevića (for group visits) 0,50 €
- Ticket for kayak users 2,00 € for the whole day
- Rental of kayaks from National Park (one-seat) 3 € for one hour; Rental of kayaks (two-seat) 5 € for one hour
- Use of guide services 60 € for 4 hours and 100 € for 8 hours

- Camping: Use of space for setting up a tent 3,00 € for one day; Use of Caravan 3,00 € for one day; Use of decorated camping space 10,00 € / day

National Park Prokletije is the youngest National Park in Montenegro. It covers the area of **Plav** district and has a total surface of 16630 ha, while the elevation is 2000 meters. The climate is continental, mountain and subalpine. The winters are very sharp and long, and the summers are fresh and short. Average annual air temperature of 2-7 ° C. The maximum amount of precipitation is excreted in late autumn and the first part of winter. The snow cover is an average thickness of 15cm and it lasts for 90 - 210 days.

The dominant characteristic of this region is the richness and diversity of the flora and fauna, so this area is one of the centers of Balkan highland diversity. National Park Prokletije is rich in larger and watercourses, hot springs and sources of potable and mineral water, rivers, underground editions. The area is rich in lakes, among which are the most popular: **Hridsko, Visitorsko, Ropojansko, Tartarsko, Bjelajsko. Hridsko Lake**, with the area of about 35 000 m2 at 1970 m, belongs to the highest and, in many opinions, the most beautiful lake in Montenegro. With its beauty, the **Visitorsko Lake** stands at 1820 meters, with a grassy floating island - spruce in the middle, which in the past served as a habitat for animals from mountain beasts. The specificity of this National Park is made up of over 1,700 species of plants, which represents half of the flora of Montenegro, or about one-fifth of the total Balkan flora. National Park Prokletije is rich in forests, among which are dominated by hardwoods and softwoods. Almost half of the forest wealth has a rainforest. In the biogeographical view of Prokletije, they belong to the Alpine-mountain region, which also had an impact on the animal world, which is characterized by great diversity. In this area live rabbit, wolf, brown bear, lynx, wild boar, wild boar, deer, and 161 recorded species of birds. Their habitats are highland regions, the valleys of Ropojan and Grbaje, forest ecosystems, mountain lakes, and rivers.

Relief of Prokletije is razed, with numerous heights, cliffs, steep slopes, river valleys of the alpine type and other natural phenomena. Due to the specific relief conditions, it is not advisable to visit National Prokletije without an expert who will follow you around. Those who wish to climb are advised to hire a professional. Activities such as climbing, hiking, cycling, riding and walking tours are available for everyone. National Park Prokletije represents a special place in Montenegro, with wild and untouched nature and beautiful landmarks.

National Park Prokletije can be reached by bus from Plav to Gusinje, or by car.

USEFUL INFORMATION:

- Entrance fee for National Park Prokletije (including visits to the Visitor Center, Educational Trails): 1,00 € (except for children under 7 years)
- Ticket for organized groups of students, students, pensioners, trade union organizations and hiking associations (including visits to the Visitor Center, educational trails) - with a written request and approval from the Park Director 0,50 €

- Use of guide services 60 € for 4 hours and 100 € for 8 hours
- Rental of a tent 8,00 € for one day
- Bike Rental 5,00 € for one hour and 10 € for the whole day
- Camping: Use of space for setting up a tent 3,00 € for one day; Use of Caravan 3,00 € for one day; Use of decorated camping space 10,00 € for one day

ACTION & ADVENTURE

EVEN THOUGH YOUR VACATION IN MONTENEGRO WILL BE perfect, wherever you go or stay, there are some spots you should not miss seeing or activities you should not skip. Here is the list of some of them:

Tara Rafting A thing you should definitely not miss in Montenegro is rafting through the most wonderful gorge and one of the longest canyons, not in Europe, but in the whole World! The sources of turquoise waters take the breath of visitors, and those who are searching for an adrenaline rush are impressed with the scenery this place has to offer. Tara river is known through the World as the „Tear of Europe ", and this is certainly due to the priceless beauty and its crystal-clear waters. The valley of Tara is a true paradise on Earth, with stone and pebble terraces engraved in rocks and surrounded by forests and greenery. The surrounding of the valley hides more than 80 big caves. Most of them are still untouched and unexplored, and in some of them were found traces of prehistoric life. It's no surprise that Tara was listed as World Natural Heritage. Rafting on

Tara, however, is an unforgettable experience – something you cannot experience every day, or everywhere.

There are numerous agencies that offer arrangements for rafting on Tara and please make sure to do this with the help of a professional!

Ostrog Monastery This beautiful Monastery that is located on the main road from Podgorica to Niksic is worldwide famous for its miracles. The stunning beauty and the scenery complement the popularity of this place. The Monastery is built in the stones and has a fascinating architecture. Many people from all around the World come here to pray to St. Vasilije Ostroski – no matter what age, religion, race, nationality.

Nevidio Canyon Popular canyon for commercial canyoning and has a great number of visitors each year. It was conquered only in 1965, and, since then, it attracts everyone. Nevidio Canyon is a unique tourist attraction, full of astonishing beauty, cascades and sparkling water. This jewel of Montenegro is found 50 km from Zabljak and 55 km from Niksic. Even though there is no special physical condition required for visitors, it is recommended to pass through the canyon with a professional guide. It is not recommended for claustrophobic people, or for minors. Those who want to experience canyon should note that once they begin cruising, there is no turning back until the path is over. The passage season starts in July - if the water level of the Komarnica river is lower, then somewhat earlier, and ends in September. However, if the weather conditions permit, the season can be extended slightly. After heavy rains, there is a danger of torrential rains and higher water levels. The adventure in Nevidio Canyon usually lasts two to three hours and requires adequate equipment - a long diving suit of at least 5 mm thick (due to the extremely low water temperature of seven to eight degrees), footwear, and helmet.

Adventure Park Lovcen This park is intended for all ages and all levels of physical wellness and conditions. It is located in National Park Lovcen at Ivanova Korita resort (Cetinje municipality). Each activity in the Adventure Park is fully safe and visitors will be welcomed by trained professionals. There are numerous tracks (lines) specially designed for each age. This place is a perfect location for all kinds of visitors: individuals, groups of friends, couples, families with children, sports teams, etc.

Kitesurfing The biggest kitesurfing center of the whole Balkans is located at Ada Bojana. Kitesurfing combines different sports (such as wakeboarding, snowboarding, surfing, sailing, paragliding, and windsurfing) and represents an ideal opportunity for all lovers of extreme sports. Ulcinj and its Ada Bojana is the perfect place for kitesurfing as it has a huge sandy shoreline (more than 14 km long), great breeze conditions and ideal climate. Kitesurfing professionals, sports teams and organizations will be pleased to welcome you and assist you on this unforgettable experience. Kitesurfing on Ada Bojana is suitable even for amateurs in this extreme sport, as the local professionals will guide you and assist you. The most famous kitesurfing spots in Ada Bojana are: Kitesurf Club Dolcinium, Ka'banya, Kiteloop, Sandbox Beach, Copacabana

Jeep Safari Zabljak Montenegro is the country that has more than 1000 km of rough terrain and is ideal for jeep safari. Many agencies and jeep safari clubs organize routes that include not only jeep safari but walking tours and enjoyment of surrounding landscapes. The prices range from

10 to 30 euros, depending on the number of people. The most popular agency is the Jeep Safari Durmitor Tours.

MONTENEGRO'S HIDDEN GEMS

Even though Montenegro is called "the hidden gem of Europe", the country itself hides many treasures that are still unexplored and not commercialized. Here is the list of some undiscovered gems within the beautiful country of Montenegro:

Morinj

Small fishing village located 30 km from Kotor to Herceg Novi. It is placed down in the fjord, at the foot of Risan sides and the vertical mountain cornice. During the summer, Morinj is all covered in the sun, but during the winter time, there are days with no sun at all. Morinj is a unique sea place with a clean beach and crystal water. The place can be reached from Kotor either by car, taxi, bus, or boat.

Dobre vode

A small settlement located 8 km from Bar. This place is a true air spa, combining different breezes blowing from the mountain and the ocean. Dobre vode is particularly recommended for those fighting with asthma, bronchitis or any other respiratory disease. This small sea diamond is a perfect getaway from noisy summer cities. The place is reachable by car, taxi or bus either from Bar or Ulcinj.

Crvena stijena (Red rock) Beach

This hidden gem is located behind the Volujica hill in Bar. This is definitely one of the most amazing beaches on the Montenegrin seaside, but still unknown even for many locals. Crvena stijena beach is isolated and has crystal-clear water. The beach can be reached from Budva or Bar (car or bus), then by walk.

Canyon Medjurec

On the southern slopes of Rumija, you will find a fascinating Canyon Medjurec, still unexplored even by locals. The scenery in the canyon will leave everyone breathless. The passage through Canyon Medjurec is recommended only to experienced professionals, while amateurs or recreationists can still enjoy some parts of it. Canyon Medjurec can be reached by car or bus (and then by walk). Access is from the main road that leads from Bar to Ulcinj.

Kucka korita and Bukumirsko Lake

Visiting Podgorica can be uninteresting for some, but a perfect getaway is definitely to the surrounding of the city – Kucka Korita and Bukumirsko Lake. Bukumirsko Lake is just 50 km away from Podgorica and hides unbelievable nature and beautiful landmarks. Many tourists decide to take a walking tour around Kucka Korita and then visit Bukumirsko Lake. This can be done with the help of travel agencies or guided hiking professionals. Kucka Korita and Bukumirsko Lake are accessible by car or bus, from the direction of Podgorica.

Visoravan Lukavica

This hidden gem is located only 30 km from Niksic. Visoravan Lukavica is surrounded by mountains Maganik, Mali and Veliki Zurim and Borovik. In this area, you will find two beautiful and still unexplored lakes, Manito and

Kapetanovo Lake. Visoravan Lukavica is an ideal place for all nature lovers or for those who wish to disconnect from everyday life. The place is reachable from Niksic, by car or taxi. Taxi fees are not high, which is a significant benefit of visiting this natural treasure.

Montenegro cities from A-Z

Andrijevica, Bar, Berane, Bijelo Polje, Budva, Cetinje, Danilovgrad, Herceg Novi, Kolasin, Kotor, Mojkovac, Niksic, Plav, Pljevlja, Pluzine, Podgorica, Rozaje, Savnik, Tivat, Tuzi, Ulcinj, Zabljak, Gusinje, Petnjica

Montenegro is an independent country located in southeastern Europe on the Balkan Peninsula. The territory of Montenegro occupies approximately 13,812 km^2. Montenegro has 625.266 inhabitants. The capital city is Podgorica. It is a "civic, democratic, ecological state of social justice based on the reign of Law" stated by the Constitution of Montenegro. The official name is the Republic of Montenegro. The currency in use is Euro. At the same time, Montenegro is a Mediterranean country and a mountainous area. Due to this fact, the climate is colorful, diverse and adaptable.